Stop Talking, Start Doing!

Attracting People of Color to the Library Profession

Gregory L. Reese

Ernestine L. Hawkins

American Library Association

Chicago and London

1999

Text and cover design by Dianne M. Rooney

Composition by the dotted i in Jansen Text and Bauer Bodoni using Quark 3.32

Printed on 50-pound white offset, a pH-neutral stock, and bound in 10-point coated cover stock by McNaughton & Gunn

The paper used in this publication meets the minimum requirements of American National Standard for Information Sciences—Permanence of Paper for Printed Library Materials, ANSI Z39.48-1992. ∞

Library of Congress Cataloging-in-Publication Data

Reese, Gregory L.
    Stop talking, start doing! : attracting people of color to the library profession / Gregory L. Reese & Ernestine L. Hawkins.
        p.   cm.
    Includes bibliographical references and index.
    ISBN 0-8389-0762-8 (alk. paper)
    1. Minority librarians—Recruiting—United States.   I. Hawkins, Ernestine L.   II. Title.
Z682.4.M56R44   1999
023'.9—dc21   99-18329

Printed in the United States of America.

03   02   01   00   99   5   4   3   2   1

To
Dr. E. J. Josey
and other pioneers
in the field of library
and information science
who have paved
the way

Contents

Preface

This publication is intended to demonstrate the importance of having a racially and ethnically diverse workforce within the library profession. Recruiting people of color to our profession is a difficult task. This work will provide recommended strategies that will enhance the recruitment process.

Changing demographics are having a significant effect on the workforce, and recent research reveals that women and minorities will be entering the labor pool in increasing numbers into the next century. Library administrators and employee trainers must develop new skills in order to work effectively with the many new types of employees, such as understanding how it feels to be different and establishing a common ground with minority employees.

Marketing the profession as a viable career option to the racial and ethnic minority population is a sure way to increase interest in the profession. We strongly contend that members of the minority community have not selected library and information science as a career option due to limited exposure to the profession. Successful recruiting of people of color begins with our young people. We as library professionals must tap the minority student bodies of our junior and senior high schools as well as those in undergraduate programs across the country.

The schools of library and information science should reaffirm their commitment to increasing minority access to the library and information science profession by adopting a comprehensive program for the recruitment of minorities. While there has been limited progress toward achieving a modicum of access for people of color, the continuing severe underrepresentation of minorities in the library and information science profession remains one of the most pressing problems that we are facing today.

We extend our appreciation to ALA Editions for providing the opportunity to work on such an important and timely issue that confronts our profession. Being African American and very active within the profession has afforded us the opportunity to witness how the lack of ethnic diversity has affected the library profession and the library community in general.

We recognize that much of the information contained in this work refers to the African American experience within the library profession, and we are cognizant of the fact that other minority groups have experienced many of the same difficulties in navigating the maze of the profession as well. However, the African American experience must be more prominent in this work because it is the area in which the most glaring inequities have come to light and where we feel the most ground has yet to be gained.

We sincerely appreciate the recent progress the American Library Association has demonstrated in the area of minority recruitment, yet much more needs to be done. We hope that this document will serve as a reference tool, a resource that provides direction for those within our profession who sincerely seek to find avenues to diversify our profession.

Gregory L. Reese
Ernestine L. Hawkins

Acknowledgments

Special thanks to the American Library Association and especially Marlene R. Chamberlain, Senior Acquisitions Editor/ALA Editions, whose expertise was invaluable in the preparation of this publication.

We also appreciate the support and assistance received from the following individuals, organizations, and institutions:

E. J. Josey, Professor Emeritus
School of Information Sciences
University of Pittsburgh

Sandra Balderrama, Diversity Officer
American Library Association

Satia Orange, Director
Office for Literacy and Outreach Services
American Library Association

Florence Simkins Brown, Director
North Miami Beach Public Library
Founder, Stop Talking and Start Doing Recruitment Workshops

Gerald G. Hodges, Director
Chapter Relations Office
American Library Association

Kathleen de la Peña McCook, Director/Professor
School of Library and Information Science
University of South Florida

Em Claire Knowles, Assistant Dean
School of Library and Information Science
Simmons College

Andrew A. Venable Jr., Deputy Director
Cleveland Public Library, Cleveland, Ohio

Maurice Wheeler, Director
Detroit Public Library, Detroit, Michigan

Acknowledgments

Alex Boyd, Past President
Black Caucus of the American Library Association

Ellen M. Stepanian, Library Media Director
Shaker Heights City Schools, Shaker Heights, Ohio

Camila A. Alire, Dean
School of Library and Information Science
Colorado State University

George C. Grant, Past President
Black Caucus of the American Library Association

John C. Tyson, Past President
Black Caucus of the American Library Association

Stanton F. Biddle, Past President
Black Caucus of the American Library Association

Sylvia Sprinkle-Hamlin, Immediate Past President
Black Caucus of the American Library Association

Organizations

Asian/Pacific American Librarians Association (APALA)

Black Caucus of the American Library Association (BCALA)

National Association to Promote Library Services
to the Spanish Speaking (REFORMA)

Chinese-American Librarians Association (CALA)

American Indian Library Association (AILA)

Ohio Library Council

The State Library of Ohio

Chapter Relations Office of ALA

The Board of Trustees, East Cleveland Public Library

The Cleveland Area African American Library Association (CAALA)

Institutions

Kent State University, School of Library and Information Science

East Cleveland Public Library and Staff

University of Pittsburgh, School of Information Sciences

Introduction

A recent report by the Census Bureau describes an American population that already has changed a great deal and by the year 2020 will have changed a great deal more. Hispanics will be the second-largest minority, overtaking African Americans, and the white population will continue its decrease as a percentage of the population. Libraries, like every other American business, will be affected by these changes. People, after all, are what markets are made of. And as the demographics shift, as markets shift, libraries that provide entertainment, educational, and cultural services to the American public may find that the makeup of their workforce does not effectively reflect the market they serve. And that can be more than a public relations disaster; it can be a financial one as well.

Minority Markets and Minority Recruitment

It is an interesting challenge for the library profession that traditionally has been dominated by white, affluent, and well-educated members of our society to figure out how to develop new markets. Will an overwhelmingly white library field continue its present course, attracting neither minority workers to its employ nor ethnic minority audiences to its services?

Of course, many in the library industry agree that there should be more minorities in the business. However, when the question changes to why this state of affairs exists, and whether or not anything can or should be done about it, the answers are tellingly various. Some feel there are cultural, if not racial, biases among library professionals; others contend that there are indeed racial causes. And still others conclude that it is a mystery why there aren't more non-white people in the library business.

Librarianship is a rather fortunate business in that it seldom has to recruit people. Libraries large and small are besieged with applications from hundreds of eager white library professionals who are recent graduates of our nation's library schools. Many library professionals have decided that ethnic minorities in general and African Americans in particular just do not seem interested in the library profession.

The issue of ethnic minority recruitment to librarianship has been slightly addressed previously by the American Library Association and a handful of concerned library professionals and educators. While there is a growing interest and awareness of the issue, the percentages of ethnic minority students seeking library and information science as a career have been minimal. The recruitment of ethnic minorities to the profession represents a complex problem that is tied to social, economic, and educational policies.

The intent of this work is to provide library educators and practitioners with strategies that will assist in the recruitment of ethnic minorities to the field of library and information science. This project will address the changing demographic trends in America and point out the significance of a diverse workforce of library professionals to address the information needs of our ethnically diverse communities.

Statistical data will provide the reader with startling figures regarding faculty staffing, student enrollment, and completion of graduate programs by ethnic minorities at accredited schools of Library and Information Science. Recommended changes in the academic environment designed specifically to recruit ethnic minorities to library schools across the country will also be examined.

Marketing the profession as a positive and socially valuable career choice is extremely important when addressing the issue of ethnic minority recruitment. This work will present new and effective methods of marketing our profession designed to attract the attention of young adults, undergraduate students, and adults searching for a viable choice as a second career. We will also suggest how the American Library Association along with state and local library organizations can work collaboratively to address the issue of ethnic minority recruitment and retention.

The American Library Association

The American Library Association (ALA), the largest library-advocacy group and the moral center of the profession, is the logical leader for new initiatives to expand the ranks of ethnic knowledge navigators and to bring about cultural diversity in our libraries and digital communities. The potential exists for an inclusive, all-color, professional cadre of expert knowledge navigators to provide new communities of new populations with quality library and information services.[1]

Introduction

Any diversity initiative envisioned requires the collaboration of ALA-accredited library-education institutions, interested members, and the wider community in order to attract minorities to the profession. All recommendations provided in this work need the support and cooperation of individual library professionals and the American Library Association as an organization. The process of attracting people of color and bringing more minorities into the workforce must be an ongoing collaborative effort that is supported by the profession as a whole and not just promoted by those of us who understand its importance or those who currently represent the minority population of library and information science professionals.

ALA's Spectrum Initiative will be discussed along with other initiatives that can only be effective if the majority of our membership recognizes the need and embraces the effort to make the needed changes occur.

It is our firm belief that if there is going to be any significant change in the representation of ethnic minorities within the workforce of library and information science, we as library professionals and as an organization (American Library Association) of committed professionals must initiate and wholeheartedly support the process.

America's largest ethnic minority populations—African American, Asian/Pacific Islander, Latino/Hispanic, and Native American—make up about 26 percent of the population but only 10.5 percent of library school graduates.

The library profession as a whole is losing ground in recruiting to and educating minorities for library and information science professions while the ethnic makeup of the nation continues to change. ALA must do what other professions such as teaching, medicine, and engineering have been doing for years—mount an effective initiative that will noticeably increase the numbers of people of color in the profession.

Increasing the number of minority librarians is beneficial to the total workforce in all communities. More minority librarians in the workforce help all personnel become more attuned to issues of diversity and thus improve the quality of service to minority and other communities.

The trained staff necessary to plan and deliver services to these growing population groups and who are informed about their cultures, knowledgeable of their languages, and familiar with their life experiences are not currently available in sufficient numbers, nor is there any indication that this will change.

A special thank you to E. J. Josey, Elizabeth Martinez, Betty Turock, the Office for Literacy and Outreach Services (OLOS), and the ethnic caucuses of the American Library Association and all other long-time advocates of minority recruitment who have made major contributions toward the library education of ethnic minorities.

Spectrum Initiative

Hats off to former ALA Executive Director Elizabeth Martinez and all those who have supported the American Library Association's "Spectrum Initiative." The initiative, a strategically planned and organized effort to recruit ethnic minorities to the library profession, is supported by the American Library Association. And from all indications, this organized effort to address the issue of recruitment has been successful. The Spectrum Initiative has done more to recruit ethnic minorities to library schools within a very limited span of time than has taken place ever before. The Spectrum Initiative is a three-year program designed to invite schools of library and information science to form a consortium for the purpose of educating a total of 50 students per year representing the four largest ethnic minority populations—African Americans, Asian/Pacific Islanders, Latino/Hispanics, and Native Americans. Students receive scholarships of no less than $5,000 per year to attend a master's degree program at one of the consortium schools. Each consortium school receives $30,000 per year to carry out a variety of enrichment activities for the students. An ALA staff team coordinates the initiative, developing a national recruitment network and working with an advisory committee. An annual leadership institute is held for graduates and midcareer minority librarians to meet and discuss issues of diversity with library leaders. The Spectrum Initiative is being funded with $1.5 million from the ALA Future Fund.[2]

The Spectrum Initiative is the first significant effort to recruit people of color with the goal of diversifying the library and information science profession. When one notes the history of the American Library Association, the issue of recruiting minorities to the library profession has clearly never been a priority. The Spectrum Initiative is a step in the right direction, yet it cannot provide the level of support needed to make a significant impact on the minority recruitment process. More dollars and more sensitivity must be garnered to truly diversify our ranks within the profession.

The American Library Association has engaged in a program that will ensure quality library and information services for an entire spectrum of Americans. ALA can expand this effort to address services to our diverse communities by initiating additional programs that respond specifically to the underrepresentation of minority library and information professionals.

Chapter Relations Office

The Chapter Relations Office of the American Library Association, currently directed by Gerald G. Hodges, promotes a sense of identification between the national Association and the 57 ALA chapters. It facilitates communication between the chapters and all ALA units by coordinating leadership development for chapter officers, chapter councilors, chief paid staff members, and other chapter leaders. The Chapter Relations Office strengthens membership promotion activities for ALA and the chapters; it also coordinates the ALA Student Chapters and helps raise awareness of and sensitivity to chapter needs throughout the American Library Association.

At the American Library Association's Annual Conference held in 1994, the Chapter Relations Committee introduced the first "Stop Talking, Start Doing" ethnic minority recruitment workshop. The workshop has been conducted at each Midwinter and Annual ALA conference since that time. This truly invigorating workshop is the brainchild of Florence Simkins Brown, director of the North Miami Beach Public Library. Each workshop is designed to introduce ways in which we as library professionals can strengthen efforts to encourage the recruitment of ethnic minorities to the library profession. Distinguished guest presenters provide innovative approaches to the issue of minority recruitment that respond to the question "How can I assist with the recruitment effort?" Stop talking about the issue of ethnic minority recruitment and start formulating some new and creative ways to address this extremely important issue. This recruitment effort has become so popular that Gerald, Florence, and their host of presenters have been requested to present the workshop across the country outside the ALA conferences.

Office for Literacy and Outreach Services

The Office for Literacy and Outreach Services (OLOS) serves ALA by supporting and promoting literacy and equity of information access initiatives for traditionally underserved populations. These populations include new and non-readers, people geographically isolated, people with disabilities, rural and urban poor people, and people generally discriminated against because of race, ethnicity, sexual orientation, age, language, or social class.

One very important role of the Office for Literacy and Outreach Services is to ensure that the ethnic caucuses of the American Library Association are supported in their effort to ensure that the issues and concerns of ethnic minority library professionals and ethnic minority populations are properly addressed.

With the support of the OLOS office, the ethnic caucuses, which are affiliates of the American Library Association, have made significant contributions concerning issues involving ethnic minority participation in the library and information science profession. The American Library Association presently recognizes the following caucuses as affiliates:

ALA Ethnic Caucuses

Asian/Pacific American Librarians Association (APALA)

Black Caucus of the American Library Association (BCALA)

National Association to Promote Library Services to the Spanish Speaking (REFORMA)

Chinese-American Librarians Association (CALA)

American Indian Library Association (AILA)

The ethnic caucuses are national organizations of librarians dedicated to advancing the causes of ethnic minorities in the library profession. They work to improve the availability of information resources and services to minority communities throughout the nation.

The overall purposes of the ethnic caucuses are primarily the same and ensure the following:

1. To call to the attention of the American Library Association the need to respond positively on behalf of the ethnic minority members of the library profession. To also respond to the information needs of the minority community by reviewing, analyzing, evaluating, and recommending to the ALA action on the needs of minority librarians.

2. To review the records and evaluate the positions of candidates for the various offices within ALA to determine their impact upon minority librarians and services to minority communities.

3. To monitor the activities of Divisions, Round Tables and Committees of the American Library Association, by active participation within these groups, to make sure that they are meeting the needs of minority librarians.

4. To serve as a clearinghouse for information about minority librarians in promoting their wider participation at all levels of the profession and the Association.

5. To support and promote efforts to achieve meaningful communication and equitable representation in state associations and on the governing and advisory boards of libraries at state and local levels.

6. To facilitate library service which will meet the information needs of minority people.

7. To encourage the development of authoritative information resources about minorities and the dissemination of this information to the larger community.

8. To open up channels of communication to and through minority librarians in every unit of the ALA.[3]

We are delighted to see that the ethnic caucuses of the American Library Association are beginning to work as a team in addressing issues pertinent to ethnic minority recruitment and library service to minority communities. Thanks to the fine leadership of OLOS director Satia Orange, the presidents of the ethnic caucuses are beginning to communicate and share common interests regarding these issues. The ethnic caucuses are currently discussing the possibility of planning joint programs, workshops, and conferences in an attempt to enhance the effort to promote literacy and equity of information access for traditionally underserved populations. We feel that strength in numbers is an effective way to address specific goals and objectives of all the caucuses.

The Black Caucus of the American Library Association (BCALA) is currently working on an exciting project that it intends to share with other ethnic caucuses. Strength in numbers is the underlying thought process, and BCALA hopes to have this initiative under way by the annual conference of 1999. The project involves enhancing the relationship between the national organization (BCALA) and local African American library organizations around the country. We feel that a closer relationship developed between the local, state, and national ethnic minority library organizations can enhance the recruitment and services priorities of the organization. The BCALA will become an umbrella organization for local African American library organizations across the country. This exciting initiative will be spearheaded by the Affiliate/Chapters Committee of the Black Caucus of the American Library Association. We hope that our colleagues and the other ethnic caucuses recognize the importance of unifying our ranks on the local and national level and will assist in solidifying efforts to achieve our national goals and objectives in the areas of minority recruitment and service to minority communities.

The Black Caucus of the American Library Association is in the process of creating an Internet broadcast network that will connect local African American library organizations around the country with the national organization, BCALA. We will build a state-of-the-art online service that links BCALA and local African American library associations into an interactive community.

The service will provide each of the local associations with its own Web site. The Web sites will be extremely easy to maintain and will support Web publishing software. The software offers easy-entry fill-in-the-blank forms that make the creation and maintenance of Web pages so simple that it can be done by a person with only basic word processing skills—no programming skills are needed.

While easy to maintain, the Web sites will offer a host of sophisticated, interactive functions including online chatting and conferencing, radio station, newsletter, calendar, photographic album, and electronic store.

If a local organization already has a Web site, it can be provided with all the additional services without changing its present Web hosting arrangements. The BCALA and the local affiliates will all be placed on one channel on the Community Network: the BCALA channel. BCALA will have the ability to broadcast (that is put audio, graphic, text, and video messages) on the Web pages of every organization's Web site that is on the BCALA channel. In effect, we will create a fully functional broadcast network for BCALA. The whole system, Web sites and channel, will be fully secured, requiring correct passwords before information can be published on the network.

Diversity and Librarians

Probably no other profession needs sensitivity to the issues of diversity more than that of librarians. They have always been keepers of cultural wisdom, private histories, arguments, and debates. Librarians need to consider the value of having minorities in libraries today, for their benefit to the multicultural user populations as well as for the value of gaining new perspectives for the development of services, programs, and collections.[4]

Cast a wide net for minority library recruits—that is the only way in which you will get enough. Send professional librarians to recruit on various campuses—but with greater effort. Many businesses try to get to minority talent even earlier. They provide summer internships and year-round management programs for minority college students. The young people learn about the company while they get valuable job experience—and managers can look prospects over before they make an offer.

The recruitment of minorities to the field of Library and Information Science is imperative. The manner in which we as library professionals embark upon this challenge should be of significant importance to all library professionals across the nation. This work simply attempts to present some suggested ways in which we as library professionals can promote the recruitment process.

NOTES

1. Elizabeth Martinez, "Diversity: The Twenty-First-Century Spectrum," *American Libraries* 28 (March 1997): 32.

2. Elizabeth Martinez, "Spectrum Initiative, an initiative of the American Library Association, to encourage and provide assistance to those pursuing careers in library and information science," Feb. 1997.

3. Mission and Purposes of the Black Caucus of the American Library Association. Home page: http://www.bcala.org/bcala.html

4. Stuart C. A. Whitwell, "Intimate World, Intimate Workplace: How the Association of Research Libraries and ALA Are Strengthening Their Commitment to Diversity," *American Libraries* 27 (Feb. 1996): 56.

1

The Browning of America

Libraries are fundamental to the American educational experience. Libraries can be very effective and dynamic learning centers for everyone and contribute to helping the nation's ethnic minority communities achieve the National Education Goals. How all Americans perceive the role of the information specialist and public libraries in their lives is of extreme importance. Ethnic minorities, especially African and Hispanic Americans, regard public libraries as a very important source of support for their communities' educational aspirations. Also, statistics indicate that the lower the education and income level of people, the higher they rate the educational importance of their public library. The eight major roles of the public library in ethnic minority communities are as follows:

1. Educational support center for students of all ages
2. Learning center for adult independent learners
3. Discovery and learning center for preschool children
4. Research center for scholars and researchers
5. Center for community information
6. Information center for community business
7. Comfortable, quiet place to read, think, or work
8. Center of recreational reading of popular materials[1]

We as library professionals must address issues regarding the changing demographics within our society and make the needed alterations in the overall structure of the library profession. It is our responsibility as library professionals to recognize our changing populations and to aggressively address issues that will ensure the recruitment of ethnic minority library professionals capable of providing quality library service from a cultural and intellectual perspective to our ethnic minority communities.

U.S. policymakers are beginning to acknowledge the growing disparities in our society. While the U.S. standard of living is the highest in the world, the experience of millions of ethnic minority citizens is one of inadequate housing, poverty-level incomes (whether employed or unemployed), illiteracy, and low educational attainment. It is very unfortunate that our institutions of higher education, library service, and the profession itself mirror the racism and limited access to economic and educational opportunities present in the larger society.[2] The problem of recruitment in the profession will not be resolved in isolation. Immediate and long-range strategies must be developed in the context of broader social issues. Demographic patterns, changes in the academic environment, and racial and ethnic attitudes are key issues addressed in this work, and these issues constitute the broader context for the recruitment of minority people into the profession.

As long ago as in the fall 1991 issue of *Library Administration & Management*, in the article "Recruiting the Underrepresented: Collaborative Efforts between Library Educators and Library Practitioners," Em Claire Knowles and Linda Jolivet were discussing changing demographics and the importance of recruiting more ethnic minorities to the library profession. "People of color need to be trained in the library and information profession, not to serve only their own communities but to serve all communities. Librarians of color are crucial to the provision of services in communities where knowledge of the language, the values, and the cultural heritage of the growing racial and ethnic minority communities is imperative."[3]

By the year 2000, 80 percent of the U.S. workforce will be minorities, women, and people from other countries. Right now, over 50 percent of the workforce is made up of women and minorities; 20 percent are immigrants. By year 2010, white men will account for less than 40 percent of the total American workforce. Women and people of color will fill 75 percent of the 24 million new jobs created in the United States.

If current trends in immigration and birth rates persist, the Hispanic population will have further increased an estimated 21 percent, the Asian presence about 22 percent, African Americans 12 percent, and whites little more than 2 percent when the twentieth century ends. It is estimated that by the year 2000, the nation's collective minority population (Blacks, Hispanics, Asians, and Native Americans) will have reached 71 million, or 26.2 percent of the total U.S. population. Between 1990 and 2000, the minority population is expected to increase by 20 percent, compared with a 7.4 percent increase for the nation's population as a whole.

By year 2020, a date no farther into the future than Martin Luther King's assassination is in the past, the number of U.S. residents who are Hispanic or non-white will have more than doubled, to nearly 115 million, while the white population will not have increased at all. By 2058, when someone born today will be 60 years old, the "average" U.S. resident, as defined by the census statistics, will trace his or her descent to Africa, Asia, the Hispanic world, the Pacific Islands, Arabia—almost anywhere but white Europe. Educating, training, and managing this increased workforce diversity is already posing a tremendous challenge for educational institutions as well as other governmental, industrial, and major business organizations throughout the United States.[4]

The traditional dependence on smokestack, goods-producing manufacturing industries that has sustained the economy for most of the century and ensured world leadership since World War II is shifting toward an economy focused on creating knowledge and providing services that requires of its workers higher levels of education and technical skills for full participation. The "technology boom" that is partially responsible for transforming American society from a manufacturing to a service-dominated economy will create 25 million more jobs by the year 2000 than were available in 1985, with minorities projected to occupy 29 percent of the new jobs, provided they are properly educated to do so.[5]

Among these new jobs, the most rapid growth is projected at the top of the job hierarchy, in the major occupational categories of professional specialties, which include physical sciences, engineering, life sciences, social sciences, and college and university teaching. All of these usually require the highest level of educational preparation, the doctorate. Projected to grow by 3.5 million jobs between 1988 and 2000 (an increase of 24 percent), the professional specialty occupational categories will continue their rapid growth and increase their share of all occupations from 12.4 percent in 1988 to 13.3 percent by the end of the century.

Without a doubt, our society is changing rapidly. Over the next ten years, the American workplace demographics will continue to undergo dramatic shifts—away from the European-American male majority of the past toward a far more diverse and segmented population of the future.[6]

Labor Shortage

One important implication of our changing demographics is the very real potential for a labor shortage. Managers are expected to experience increasing difficulty in meeting their staffing needs. Primarily, this is because the individuals composing the bulk of the workforce growth historically have been underrepresented in the occupations where the greatest growth is expected. This includes the business of disseminating information, library and information science.

Skills Gap

According to current trends, managers of all organizations can anticipate a time when the potential labor force will consist of large numbers of minorities and women who will be willing and physically able to work but will lack the necessary skills to take advantage of occupational opportunities. This scenario has been called the skills gap. Exacerbating this situation will be the anticipated surge in baby-boomer retirements. These combined circumstances hold the potential for a very real labor crunch.[7]

The skills of the labor force are going to be the key competitive weapon in the twenty-first century. Brainpower will create new technologies, but skilled labor will be the arms and legs that allow one to employ the new product and process technologies that are being generated. The same can be said for the labor force that will be needed to deliver efficient and effective public services. New service delivery technologies will require a skilled and educated workforce.

The critical question that policymakers, educational administrators, human resource planners, government bureaucrats, corporate leaders, and elected officials must now ask is Will this future workforce be adequately trained to meet the occupational needs of the twenty-first century, given current trends in minority participation in higher education and access to graduate and professional schools throughout America?

During the period when it was the national will to provide underrepresented minorities with increased access to higher education (the mid-to-late 1970s), minority enrollment increased in higher education and was followed by increases in degree attainment. Given this history and the trends we face, the following considerations appear logical:

- Increased minority participation in graduate and professional programs should become a national priority.
- Extensive training systems for the non-college-bound should be established.

Human Investment

To take full advantage of new and emerging job opportunities and to meet the anticipated demands for employment in the nation's changing economy require a considerable investment in the development of its human capital. Such an investment needs to be of sufficient magnitude to include those segments of society that have yet to be fully represented and mainstreamed in the education process. If properly prepared, the nation's rapidly growing and increasingly youthful minority population should be well positioned to take full advantage of the expanding job opportunities that are forecast. Essentially, young minorities should be motivated to strive for higher education at an early age.

Everyone Has a Role

Minorities and women must recognize the value of skills and brainpower development and insist that educational institutions and their graduate and doctoral programs provide them with access and training. Demanding access to these programs will ensure that there will be minority and women administrators capable of managing a multicultural public and private sector labor force and serving an ethnically diverse population.[8]

Education

Educational institutions at all levels have an enormously important role to play in the proper preparation of members of society for these opportunities, especially those who have been traditionally underrepresented on the nation's campuses. A large part of that proper preparation will require institutions to reexamine existing curricula and develop educational programming that will take into account the increasing multiculturalization of the

American workforce. It appears that institutions of higher learning will have to assume at least a dual role in the development of this human capital.

First, they will have to ensure that minorities are given access to the educational process; and second, they must ensure that minorities are taught the skills that will allow them the opportunity to effectively compete in a diverse and highly competitive economic environment. This will be particularly significant for those professions that prepare individuals to serve humanity in a highly efficient manner. It will be imperative that matriculating students enter the workplace armed with the knowledge that they will be serving a multicultural clientele and that success in serving this diverse population is contingent upon cultural sensitivity and valuing differences.

The impact of these changing demographics on the American workforce is problematic, but it is certain that this "browning of America" will alter everything in society, from politics and education to industry, values, and culture. These demographic shifts will affect hiring practices, admissions policies, educational curricula, training policies, and service delivery systems. The challenges that these changes pose for the public sector are significant, due in part to the delicate balance between quality of life, human well being, and public service policy and programming.

As America moves into the twenty-first century, it carries with it significant and major transformations in the way goods will be produced, the type of goods produced, and the extent and type of services produced and delivered. The relative decline of industrial manufacturing and growth of the service sector have led some social scientists to note that America has been shifting from an industrial to a post-industrial or service economy. This trend has also been described as a shift from an industrial to an information society.

Whether we call it an information, post-industrial, or service economy, the fact is that almost all the new jobs in this country are presently and will most likely continue to be in the information, knowledge, and service sectors. A worldwide revolution has occurred in the technologies of goods production, information processing, and communications. Automation and technological change have marginalized labor-intensive industries and created new challenges for America in responding to global market pressures and attempting to maintain its world leadership and economic competitiveness.

Diversity became an issue when three powerfully significant trends reached their own critical points at about the same time:

1. The global market in which American corporations must now do business became intensely competitive.
2. The makeup of the U.S. workforce began changing dramatically, becoming more diverse.
3. Individuals increasingly began to celebrate their differences and become less amenable to compromising what makes them unique. This inclination represents a marked departure from previous times when predispositions were to "fit in."

Adequate preparation of minorities for public service in the twenty-first century requires that American colleges and universities structure public service educational programs to train minority administrators capable of managing a multicultural workforce and serving an ethnically diverse population.

Educating minorities for public service in the immediate future is imperative. Minorities who possess graduate degrees will be asked to manage multicultural public service agencies such as libraries and to serve an ethnically diverse population. Changing demographics in the United States are increasing the need for library services to ethnic groups. Most library programs do not yet make mainstream library activities available to multicultural populations. Essentially, minority youth should be motivated to strive for higher education at an early age. We as library professionals need to introduce library and information science as a viable career option for minority students throughout the nation.

The library and information science profession must position itself for the developments being brought forth demographically within our society. If we plan to continue as forerunners in the information business, we must seriously evaluate how we will deliver effective library service in the immediate future and who will deliver it.

NOTES

1. U.S. Dept. of Education, Office of Educational Research and Improvement, Library Programs, "Public Libraries Serving Communities: Education Is Job #1," Washington, D.C., 1994.
2. Ann Knight Randall, *Minority Recruitment in Librarianship: Librarians for the New Millennium* (Chicago: Office for Library Personnel Resources, ALA, 1988).

3. Em Claire Knowles and Linda Jolivet, "Recruiting the Underrepresented: Collaborative Efforts between Library Educators and Library Practitioners," *Library Administration & Management* 5 (fall 1991): 189–93.

4. Kenneth A. Jordan, Mitchell F. Rice, and Audrey Mathews, "Educating Minorities for Public Service in the Year 2000," *The Public Manager: The New Bureaucrat* 23 (summer 1994): 51.

5. Ibid., 52.

6. Ibid., 53.

7. Ibid., 58.

8. Ibid.

2

Employment Opportunities for Ethnic Minorities in the Library Field

We simply must open the doors of our profession to ethnic minorities. We hear too often that the library profession is simply inhospitable to anyone who does not fit the stereotypical librarian background: white, privileged, with cultural enthusiasms, tastes, and habits of social interaction associated with an Ivy League background.

Many African American library professionals outwardly describe the library and information science profession as one with a "hostile climate for minorities" that prevents them from feeling welcome. This criticism ranges from outrage to wry lamentation; some have commented that the profession is the "whitest industry in America."

Many in the library profession reject the notion of its being guilty of racist hiring practices, reasoning that the industry is too politically liberal for that charge to stand. Nevertheless, many ethnic minorities describe a hostile climate during interviews and employment in libraries that prevents them from feeling welcome. Ethnic minorities are beginning to speak out against the general insensitivity that the profession has projected toward minorities and their cultures.

There is a set of assumptions about minorities and a tendency to underestimate minority employees. Many white library professionals have not had exposure to the full range of ethnic minorities. It is difficult to establish your credibility when there is a mindset in which many white library professionals choose to remain ignorant of the severity of issues dealing with recruiting minorities to the profession. They sometimes totally disregard the fact that a candidate has impeccable credentials and has performed well throughout his or her career and has successfully completed the interview process.

An Exercise in Frustration

In August 1997, the Black Caucus of the American Library Association held its Third National Conference of African American Librarians in Winston-Salem, North Carolina. There were numerous workshops, lectures, and seminars that covered topics ranging from children's services and school and academic librarianship to library outreach services.

One workshop addressed the issue of minority recruitment to the library profession. There were approximately seventy individuals in attendance, and the workshop was led by four panelists who were professional librarians representing both public and academic libraries. One panelist elaborated on the many employment opportunities for people of color within the profession and stressed the importance of African Americans obtaining a degree in library and information science. A twenty-three-year-old African American woman raised her hand and interrupted the panelist just before he concluded his presentation. She angrily expressed the fact that she had recently received her degree in library and information science from Clark-Atlanta University and had searched aggressively and unsuccessfully for employment over the preceding nine months. Obviously very frustrated, she indicated that she had had absolutely no success in finding employment. "If there are so many employment opportunities out there for people of color, why am I having such difficulty in finding a job?"

All attention was directed toward this young woman as she began to explain her disappointment with the interview process involved while applying for various library positions at many different libraries. She stressed the fact that while being interviewed, she repeatedly encountered a feeling of rejection by those conducting the interview. Whether it was a group or an individual, in each instance she felt that she was being scrutinized unfairly or simply being treated differently because she was African American. All interviewers were white, and the same sense of hostility seemed to fill the room during each and every interview. "From the unfriendly looks on their faces and the abrupt manner in which they conducted the interview, I knew within the first three minutes of the process that I was not the candidate to be seriously considered for the position. I got the impression that the entire interview process was a waste of time. Maybe I should have considered some other career, because the opportunities are certainly not there for African American librarians." Minority members of the audience responded with applause, many of them having endured similar experiences while interviewing for positions within predominantly white library organizations or institutions.

This experience helps illustrate that African American library professionals who possess the credentials needed to assume positions of leadership within the profession are often denied the opportunity by library boards of trustees, college deans, and human resource managers. Many African American library professionals are interviewed for positions of leadership by individuals who lack the professional skills needed to interview a candidate who is a member of an ethnic minority. Without a doubt, the applicant is treated differently, in many cases, as someone who is immediately deemed less competent.

Many recruiters conducting critical interviews often have a preconceived notion that a person of color will not meet their expectations. Selecting a person of color for the position would be too risky for the organization, or they simply decide that the person seems okay, but just might not be the "right fit" for the particular position.

"Getting Screwed"

Too often minority librarian professionals find themselves facing obstacles that have restricted their ability to ascend to management and decision-making positions. Seasoned African American library professionals have experienced this same sense of disappointment and frustration as they attempt to climb the career ladder within the world of library and information science. A very similar and disappointing experience was encountered by a seasoned African American public library director who applied for the directorship of a medium-sized library system located in the northeastern part of the country.

> Five white representatives of a seven-member board of trustees served as the search committee. The library system is located in an affluent, predominantly white community with a very stable population of approximately 34,000. The director's current position was the directorship of a medium-sized public library located within an urban poor community, predominantly African American, with an unstable and transient population of 34,000. The libraries were less than four miles from each other.

Employment Opportunities

Unfortunately, over the previous fifteen to twenty years, the African American community had been inundated with poverty, crime, and a reputation frowned upon by surrounding communities. The library director had done a superior job and was credited with resurrecting, rebuilding, and reestablishing the good reputation of the library system that was formerly plagued with poor management, resulting in a tarnished professional and public image. His many contributions to this library and the community in general had earned him several leadership awards, including the state's very distinguished Librarian of the Year award.

The director was one of nine candidates for the position of director. Eventually, the nine were reduced to three finalists, and the director made the final three. He received a call from the chairperson of the search committee, who indicated that the board had completed the interview process and that he was their top candidate. The chairperson expressed how pleased the search committee was with the interview and said that he would give the director a call within a couple of days to finalize the process. The director, very pleased to hear the positive comments, began to prepare himself for the new position. Two days later, the director did receive a call from the chairperson, who began the conversation with an apology. "I am sorry, but after further review and careful consideration, the board felt it was necessary to extend the interview process. We will advertise the position once again. Feel free to apply. We really thought you were great!" After giving the situation careful attention, the director decided that he would participate in the process once again, although he knew that his chances of securing the position were pretty unlikely.

The second interview was a nightmare. It was quite clear that the board had already decided that the director was not the person they wanted for the job. They began to interview applicants with significantly less experience than the director, and the process took three months to complete. It was evident that the board did not want to grant this African American male from the poor side of town the opportunity to serve as their library director. During the final interview, one of the board members asked, "Just because you have been successful in your present community, what makes you think you can be successful here?" It was clear that the board member felt that the director could serve successfully in the poor community made up of predominantly African Americans but would not be capable of serving as director in the predominantly white and wealthy community. Prior successes or how much experience the director possessed made no difference, he was just not the person for the job. The entire process became very unprofessional and embarrassing for all involved, especially for the director. It was his fourth month of being involved in the interview process.

The interview process was so extensive and unprofessional that eventually the director's board of trustees at his home library heard of his application to the neighboring library and began to question his commitment to his current position and library. Rumors began to circulate, and the situation became a circus. The director received numerous letters of support and telephone calls from residents of the wealthy community who knew the director was being treated unfairly. One call came from a resident who indicated that her niece was a staff member at the library and that rumors surrounding the director's appointment were rampant. Based on rumors only, she shared with the director the reasons why he was not being considered for the position. Number one, he was an African American male who might pose a threat to the white female staff. Secondly, they felt he might attempt to convert the library from a highly respected traditional library setting into an Afrocentric cultural center that would feature monthly jazz concerts and semiannual barbecues held on the front lawn of the library.

The director also received letters from the African American segment of the community indicating their support and embarrassment over the entire situation. They suggested that the director consider a lawsuit.

Of course, the director was not selected. The board selected a white male who was an assistant director of a library system outside the state. The director chalked the experience up as another unsuccessful battle in a society of racist individuals who feel that African Americans are not as capable of performing a job as well as whites. To take any form of legal action would probably have caused the director additional aggravation. A white colleague and long-time resident of the wealthy community personally contacted the director to express his disappointment and embarrassment with the entire process. He extended an apology for his entire community. He also made it very clear that he would have loved to have the director serve as top administrator of his home library. His final comment to the director was, "Man, you really got screwed!"

At this writing, there are only seven or eight African American men and fourteen to seventeen African American women who are public library directors within the United States. Over the years, there has been no concerted effort to increase these numbers, so the figures have remained relatively constant.

The Progressive Library

The new litmus test of the progressive organizations of the future will be reflected not only by how well they recruit and attract minorities but also whether their corporate culture truly values diversity and views it as an asset.

Tangible evidence of whether diversity is valued in an organization is the ability of its managers to build and motivate effective work teams and to avoid stereotypical assumptions in assigning work to these teams. This requires the organization to encourage its managers to actively extend themselves to people who are different. By doing so, the organization's managers learn about others and their individual differences. In the process, managers become empowered to value diversity as an asset with the potential to enhance organizational performance through the infusion of new ideas and different perspectives. Valuing diversity translates into enhanced productivity, profitability, and competitive advantage. Specifically,

- library management must first view diversity as a business issue that affects the library industry's ability to compete effectively;
- second, library management must view diversity as a top-down initiative that requires overhauls in the library's traditional culture;
- third, library management must create an environment that reflects this commitment.

The test of such an environment will be the library industry's ability to attract and retain managers who are dedicated to making diversity work.

Those in the library profession must realize that an ethnically diverse talent pool within its infrastructure will let them connect to a diverse marketplace. Human resource planners need to make a conscious effort to change. They need to see that minority hiring is non-negotiable.

Even in a climate where there's been a backlash against affirmative action, the library profession is going to be driven by diversity. Diversity will bring library services closer to the consumer and also provide more than one perspective. People think diversity means unqualified hiring or promoting. But it's really about good business. It means being competitive.

Retention

Yet once the recruitment efforts have been made, we must also stress the importance of retention. The profession must find new ways to maintain the commitment to diversification. Retention is just as important, if not more important, than the recruitment process. It is important that once minority candidates are brought into the profession or into library schools they are allowed to express themselves as individuals and get the support from faculty, colleagues, and management that allows them to flourish.

Proactively, support groups must be formed within library institutions to give minority employees a forum within which to voice their concerns and to discuss their contributions to the organization, as well as to serve as an outlet for cultural and social support.

We must learn to become masters of our destiny in turbulent times. Most human resource development practitioners would agree that these turbulent times are a tremendous opportunity for training and development to help transform lives. That transformation includes working with and valuing others who are different.

In the 1960s, companies were forced by law to hire "different" workers (women and minorities). In the 1970s, they were told to hire physically disabled workers. As we approach the year 2000, many companies no longer have to be told; they are beginning to see the value of hiring "different" people. Companies believe seeking diversity is an asset. Valuing difference goes beyond just hiring; it must take into account differences in culture, perception, work styles, image, and function.

Library human resource planners, directors, boards of trustees of libraries, and deans and faculty of library schools at our many colleges and universities must understand what difference is and what it is not. Those who have control over hiring practices must know how to relate to difference; they must serve as role models on how to teach and live it. Knowing how to work with difference comes from personal experience and is generated by a series of emotions and thoughts.

Why do we react so negatively to people with different backgrounds, different affiliations, and different views? Is it because our minds are biologically conditioned to ignore similarities and exaggerate differences? Human beings are always, by nature, going to find it difficult to accept differences and strangeness.

The answer lies not in preaching tolerance but in getting to know one another in familiarity. The word "familiar" is, of course, related to the word "family," and it is no wonder that we feel more comfortable with someone in the family than from outside it. But the irony about "celebrating diversity" is that the more we become familiar with one another, the less we will want to celebrate. Victory will come when we learn to get less excited about differences and accept them with quiet pleasure.

Library managers need to make diversity a personal and organizational priority, self-educate, define a focus, have vision they can share, look for allies and partnerships, talk to anyone and everyone, commit resources, involve staff at all levels, create opportunities for exploration and inclusion, develop leadership, prioritize, assist and adjust, organize for clear results, and create accountability.

Before identifying objectives, two factors must be considered: What is "normal"? and How do you define "different"?

In a business such as library and information science, "normal" may be defined as doing what is expected by the majority or by administrative management. "Different" describes anything or anyone who deviates from the norm. For example, normal behavior at work in the United States may include participating in group meetings. But someone from Japan may find it difficult to openly participate in group meetings; in the Japanese culture, people are taught to listen to the instructor, teacher, or boss.[1]

The demographics have changed, both in lifestyle and in ethnicity and gender. Those changes are creating new challenges to what some people used to think of as a normal work setting. Each organization has its own norms by which to measure different people, but it is important to note the relevance of informal norms as well. Valuing difference embraces the concepts of mutual respect, acceptance of others, and the desire to work toward common goals. The nature and scope of the different worker, and issues of difference, have expanded since the 1960s. The challenge for those responsible for hiring is to develop objectives that will take into account the breadth of difference. Consider the following as objectives from which to work.

Know How It Feels

The first objective for library management is to become familiar with how it feels to be different. During seminars on working with people who are different, participants have been asked to think about times in their lives when they felt different. They are instructed to get up and walk around the room, introducing themselves with one-word descriptions of how they felt when they were different. Instead of saying "My name is Robert Jones," one might say, "Hello, my name is Awkward." That description reflects what it felt like to be different. Others may describe themselves as afraid, embarrassed, angry, frustrated, uncomfortable, scared, and lost—adjectives that are predominantly negative (though occasionally, someone has shared a positive description such as "unique"). It would be difficult to convince managers to value working with people who are "different" if they saw most of the words on that list. Difference must be reframed to bring words like "unique," "special," "talented," "gifted," "innovative," and "creative" to the forefront. Managers must become familiar with their own feelings about difference before they can be effective in helping others work with difference. It must be acknowledged at the outset that engaging in a process of understanding difference is a personal experience that does affect "the bottom line."

Find Common Ground

The second objective is to identify similar characteristics facing all people who are different. It is impossible to learn everything there is to know about every group of people. However, a particular frame of reference may help human resource practitioners embrace all difference in ways that provide opportunities to bring out the commonality of difference with all groups of people. After all, most of us want similar things such as success, love, and family. Common challenges for people who are different include language, energy, and socialization.

Language. Someone who comes to the United States from a different country may have the obvious problem of not being able to speak English. But an individual who has worked in an educational setting could have a similar problem if he or she moves into the corporate arena. The language or vocabulary of that environment—the spoken and unspoken norms— would be foreign to the person. It is a matter of learning how to translate knowledge from one culture to another.

Energy. Look at the extra energy used by a person who is different. If you are a "normal," able-bodied person, imagine the process you go through to get ready for work each day (getting dressed, making breakfast, and taking the necessary steps to transport yourself to your job). Then add in the differences you would have to contend with if you had a physical disability. Include the social concerns and reactions of others. An individual with a disability works toward company objectives, but he or she needs extra planning to get to the job, must contend with the uncertainty of colleagues regarding how to be helpful, and must deal with coworkers' curiosity. The person who is different uses extra energy to be like his or her colleagues but still feels different.

Socialization. A supervisor at a engineering company told about an employee from southeast Asia who did not understand that it was all right to converse with coworkers while on the job. Each time the supervisor said "good morning," the employee thought it meant he was not working hard enough. Hearing-impaired employees may observe two people talking together in the lunchroom and think they are talking or laughing about them. These employees were not familiar with the social aspects of work. The question for managers to ask themselves is, "How do those characteristics affect productivity and the bottom line?" Employees who are different and new to the workplace must understand the importance of planning efficiently, anticipating uncertainty of social norms, and completing job-related tasks on time. When dealing with a performance problem, the key is to be firm with consistent performance expectations, but sensitive to individual differences.

What You Can Do

The third objective is to develop strategies to increase effectiveness in working with people who are different. Be clear about the definition of "normal," about formal and informal norms, and about the kinds of differences that need to be addressed. Consider those issues individually and systemically. The steps to increasing effectiveness are easy to define but hard to implement.

Talk with someone who can help you understand the barriers you are up against when working with an individual who is different. Then go to the person who is different and say something like, "I want you to know that I have never worked with a person of color. I hope it is all right if I ask you how I can be helpful. That will help me in giving assignments and improve the working of our entire team." Read about the group of people you would like to learn more about. Articles on women, African Americans, and other groups should be included in your reading material for professional development. Get help from community resources or agencies versed in the area that you want to learn about. Most groups of different people have organizations that serve as support networks. Most groups like to maintain a sense of identity. They believe that if they join with other groups, their own individuality will be lost. For example, people of color may find it hard to affiliate with a group of people with disabilities, for fear that the issues most pertinent to their own group will not be addressed.

Consider yourself both a teacher and learner; be clear about what you do not know. If work with an individual reveals that a policy change is warranted, change it. If not, take steps to help the person understand what is expected. Some people in positions of authority confuse valuing or working with people who are different with giving away power. The truth is, working with people who are different will provide an opportunity to increase the economic base through the sharing of talents and gifts from different perspectives. The objective is to create a climate in which a message of productivity and performance prevails. If personnel policies dictate that a particular group of people must remain on the job because of their ethnicity, a manager may believe that his or her hands are tied and preferential treatment is required. Managers have the responsibility to see that a balance of sensitivity and performance is maintained.

Ways and Means

Human resource planners must identify methods for implementing a "Working with People Who Are Different" program at an organizational level. What is the readiness or need to promote change in the organization or company? It is important to note that working with difference goes beyond the Equal Employment Opportunity mandate. First, it is essential that the individual manager identify his or her own concerns about the issues and challenges surrounding the topic of difference in order to begin effective change within the organization.

Second, the manager should align difference with what is already occurring in the organization. What is the mission, or does the library even have one? It may be helpful to work from three basic assumptions:

1. We are more alike than we are different. That simply means that even though we are different, our similarities come in the pursuit of such goals as success, productivity, and teamwork.

2. Each person has something unique to offer the workplace. The positive descriptions of what it feels like to be different should be promoted to help that assumption become reality. Remember, oneness does not mean sameness. Celebrate the differences in others. Celebration can only enhance productivity and profitability in the workplace.

3. The Chinese have a two-pronged definition for the word "crisis." It can mean either danger or opportunity. We are not in danger, but we have a wealth of opportunity to serve others. Working with people who are different provides those opportunities. Human resource planners should serve as change agents in helping libraries increase their effectiveness from many perspectives.[2]

Ethnic minority librarians have encountered some truly incredible experiences while working as reference librarians within many of our public and academic libraries across the country. Being different in a library setting is no different from being unlike the majority in any other institution. The victim becomes embarrassed, angry, frustrated, uncomfortable, and very disenchanted with the entire situation.

Yes, Believe It or Not, I Am the Librarian

In numerous instances, library patrons as well as library staff of predominantly white library institutions refuse to accept the fact that the African American sitting at the reference desk and obviously employed as a professional librarian is capable of providing excellent reference service to any individual. Yet it never fails: the minority reference librarian is asked, "Do you work here?" or "Is the librarian around?" The minority librarian is situated at the reference desk with name tag and desk signage indicating that he or she is the *reference librarian*, yet many patrons refuse to acknowledge that fact and approach the white librarian for assistance. How embarrassing, how frustrating this situation becomes. In many cases, the situation becomes even more complex when the staff directs patrons to the white librarian, ignoring the minority librarian.

Skin Touching

While serving as a reference librarian, I personally encountered several interesting situations that address the issue of accepting those who are different. This particular experience involved myself and coworkers working at a library within a community that was 99.8 percent white. This community had an established reputation of being racist and very insensitive to African Americans. I was the very first African American to work at this library, and most of the staff had never experienced working with an African American, someone who was different from them. My first day was interesting. I was introduced to the staff by departments and it was one of the strangest experiences of my life. Everyone I met looked me over from head to toe, and many gave the immediate impression that they did not particularly want me there. After a few weeks, I think I was finally accepted by most of the staff. At least half began to smile when I passed them in the hallway, a great accomplishment. My first supervisory responsibility was to oversee student pages. After my third week of working with the youngsters, a few of them became quite comfortable and began to ask questions other than where to shelve a particular book. A fifteen-year-old approached me one afternoon and asked if she could touch my skin. "Greg, would you mind if I touched your skin? I've never been this close to a Black person before." This very inquisitive youngster went on to comment about her dad, "if my dad knew that I had a Black supervisor, he would make me quit this job immediately. But don't worry, I won't tell him a thing. I like working for you. He always tells us, my brothers and me, never to go downtown. He warns that Black people are downtown and you might get robbed or killed if you visit downtown."

A Well-Behaved Colored Guy

After my first three months at the same library, I began to interact with the staff and feel more comfortable. By this time, I was also becoming very familiar with the reference collection and eager to provide reference assistance. One Thursday afternoon, I was scheduled to cover the main reference desk from 1 P.M. to 4 P.M. The reference desk was located approximately twenty-five feet directly in front of the main entrance of the library. An elderly white woman entered the library about 3 P.M. and slowly made her way to the reference desk. I was informed later that this woman visited the library each and every day at approximately 3 P.M. and had been doing so for the past eleven years. Four years prior, she had become very ill and was unable to leave her home, so books and other materials were delivered to her home. This particular Thursday was her first visit to the library in four years. She slowly made her way toward the reference desk, with cane in one hand and her purse in the other. Her head was directed downward as if examining the floor. She never looked up until she was at the reference desk. She then raised her head, poised to ask for assistance. When she noticed me at the desk, she dropped her cane, brought her hand to her chest as if to grasp her heart, took a deep breath and shouted, "Oh my God, I have been away a long time!" I found the materials she requested, and she thanked me. Before she left the library, she made it a point to stop by my supervisor's office. She had known the manager for quite some time and wanted to share her impression of the service she received from the Black guy at the reference desk. My supervisor shared her comments the next day and indicated that she made the following statement, "Hey, you know that colored guy you got working at the desk out there, he found my books and he was very well behaved." I never saw the lady again. She may have passed away or decided to change libraries because of my presence.

The Hare and the Tortoise

While at the same library system, I received my first management assignment as branch manager of the only community library located within a predominantly African American population. There was a total staff of nine, seven African Americans and two whites. We once had the tedious chore of applying bar codes to the entire collection of books in preparation for automation. The job was so overwhelming that in many instances librarians from other libraries within the system were asked to assist libraries in getting the bar coding projects completed. As my white supervisor briefed six or seven white colleagues who were being assigned to assist at my branch, I was told that she clearly pointed out the fact that "The people who work at branch C are fairly nice people. We need you to go over and assist them with the bar coding project. Please don't get discouraged. They're slow but they're steady." A white colleague who was present at the briefing was so outraged by her comments that he took it upon himself to inform me of what transpired at the meeting. Later in the week, I finally decided to ask the supervisor about her comments. She replied in a very startled and nervous manner, "Yes, yes, I said that, but I did not mean it like it might have sounded." She went on to explain the tale of the hare and the tortoise and that she did not mean any harm. She apologized and left my office. I considered reporting the incident to the library director but felt it would cost me additional aggravation, so I did not pursue the situation any further. This particular incident took place at a time when I was terribly fed up with the racist remarks and frustrating experiences encountered during my tenure with the system. Within a matter of months, I sought employment with another library system, located within a predominantly African American community with African American employees. Do you think my former employer was concerned about retaining people of color? I think not.

In larger library organizations, it may be helpful to organize African, Hispanic, Asian, and Native American networks by granting them official recognition and providing a senior manager to act as mentor. These groups help new employees adjust and provide direct feedback to management on problems that concern the groups.

Combining mentoring with the issue of increasing diversity in a profession only makes good sense. The executive levels and administrations of the library profession have for far too long not been required to venture beyond their comfort zones. However, it is no longer possible to ignore the diversity of library customers and the need to make library staffs more representative of the communities they serve, whether they are on a college campus or in a neighborhood branch library.

If library professionals are serious about attracting young career-minded candidates to the field of library science, we would do well to take a serious look at the role that mentors can play in the recruitment and retention of minorities. We must emphasize the various career paths and the management opportunities available and be prepared to act as mentors to guide them on their quest for success in the library profession.

Mentors and Mentoring

The authors believe that mentoring programs can play an important role in recruiting and retaining minorities in the library profession. Our research has shown that many other professions and human resource professionals have found that mentoring is a useful tool in the struggle to find and retain young people in professions, including libraries. We would like to present some of the approaches that other professions have used in incorporating mentoring as a way to attract students and new employees to a profession.

Mentors

Mentoring is considered an important development tool in career advancement. It helps employees accomplish various business, career, and personal goals. It also assists in the identification of training and job opportunities through the provision of role models and business friendships. Moreover, mentoring programs address various issues related to organizational structure, diversity, and experiences. Some programs are designed according to cross-skill training and group, cultural, and formal needs. The process also allows minorities to overcome obstacles related to the advancement of their careers.

There is nothing new about mentoring per se. But over the years the trend has moved from the informal paradigm to a more structured format.[3] Traditionally, mentoring has been ad hoc. An older, senior member of an organization, usually white and male, would spot an up-and-comer and take it upon himself to nurture and move forward the younger worker, also usually white and male, on the track to the top. The influx of women and racial minorities into the workforce has presented both problems and opportunities for the art and craft of mentoring.

Mentoring is becoming more structured. One of the more notable approaches is the Menttium 100 program, a year-long program developed by Minneapolis-based Menttium Corp. The program matches senior-level mentors, about half of whom are male, with 100 highly motivated mid-level women from different organizations in an urban area. Originating in Minneapolis in 1991, the program now operates in Chicago, Dallas, Atlanta, and San Francisco. More than 3,000 women executives and 1,000 companies have participated in the program. The twelve-month program includes a minimum of fourteen hours of one-on-one meetings with a senior level mentor from another organization. Those being mentored also participate in monthly or quarterly discussions and lectures by experts in leadership, ethics, and conflict resolution as well as the opportunity to network with other high-potential professionals. Mentors participate at no cost, and they receive coaching from Menttium staff on maximizing their mentoring experience. Exit surveys conducted for all Menttium 100 participants show a 97 percent success rate in terms of both mentor and protégé gaining benefits from their experience.

Group mentoring is another formal approach used by some organizations. One company developed a year-long mentoring program that includes several elements. The key piece is a learning group that's made up of five or six people and a mentor. The group members, not the mentor, control both the times and frequency of their meetings. The mentor provides perspective and insights on the organizational structure, politics, and how decisions get made and why. Human resources designs the groups, looking for diversity in race, gender, educational background, and experience. The mentors, also called "learning leaders," are assigned as well. Once assembled, the groups had to work out problems themselves. The results of the program have all been positive to date. The members found out more about their areas of interest, and the mentors got more potential candidates for their various departments.

Nationsbank used mentoring to resolve the problem of having many of its talented, high-potential minority employees leave the bank. It found that, as in many other organizations, minorities often feel they don't have allies who can show them how things work and where to get help.

In response, Nationsbank inaugurated a program for twenty mentors. Most of the mentors are white males, and the forty protégés are mostly minorities. This diversity pairing challenges members of both groups to venture outside their comfort zones. The program offers one-on-one and group activities, including community discussion groups in which banking staff can explore both cross-cultural and cross-functional issues. Combining mentoring with the issue of increasing diversity highlights a potential strength of formal mentoring.

Mentoring Is a Two-Way Street

If your organization is considering a mentoring program, both parties need to clarify their expectations and roles. Some tips to help your program succeed:

ADVICE TO MENTORS

1. Let your students find their own path. All you can do is point them in the right direction.
2. People learn in different ways. Some need examples. Some need to talk over different approaches or strategies. Others need to try things out and see what works and what doesn't. Find out how the people in your group learn best and emphasize their strengths and not their weaknesses.
3. Let your students do it their way. They will have more ownership in their progress if they find their own ways to be effective.
4. Choose your words carefully. People can just as easily be confused as inspired by what you say.

ADVICE FOR MINORITY EMPLOYEES

1. Know yourself. Identify your strengths and weaknesses, which will help you and your mentor create action plans to address areas that need improvement.
2. Clarify your goals.
3. Be creative in finding a mentor. If a role model doesn't exist in your area of work, find one in another area or in another organization.

4. Stay in touch. Let your mentor know what's going on and ask for help when you need it.

5. Mentor others. One of the best ways to learn is to teach.[4]

Contemporary organizations are increasingly turning to mentoring programs as a vehicle for creating opportunities for open communication between employees and for assimilating newcomers into institutional culture. These organizations range from professional associations to educational institutions, and their initiatives range from ad hoc committees on mentoring and the adoption of resolutions on mentoring programs to the inclusion of mentoring as a strategy for achieving institutional objectives in a university's six-year plan. Because of its current popularity as an organizational socialization technique, mentoring can initially appear as a panacea, a ready solution for many organizational communication problems. However, any type of effective management of diversity requires organizational change on at least three levels: cultural, involving changes that alter the organization's basic assumptions, values, beliefs, and ideologies that define its view of itself and its environment; structural, involving changes in the grouping of positions and departments within the organization; and behavioral, involving changes in behaviors, attitudes, and perceptions among individuals and work groups. All three levels of organizational change must occur before mentoring can be implemented effectively and operated optimally.

Mentoring is a practice that serves a number of roles or functions in the workplace: mentors provide career development roles, sponsoring advancement, protecting protégés from adverse forces, providing challenging assignments, and fostering positive visibility. These activities all build on and extend reciprocal and open communication between mentor and protégé.

This relationship and the activities that occur within its boundaries ideally allow the protégés to enter and adjust to the organization with much more ease than they would be able to do without the mentor. The properly mentored employee is able to make the transition from outsider to insider more easily, to become initiated into his or her job more quickly, to establish new interpersonal relationships more effortlessly, to discover his or her role in the organization more clearly, to find congruence between self-evaluation and organizational evaluation of his or her work performance more accurately, and to resolve conflicts more readily.

Given the many benefits for both the mentor and the protégé involved in the mentoring relationship, this process is definitely one avenue for addressing the perceived inequities associated with diversity in the workplace.

In spite of the benefits of such relationships, barriers sometimes inhibit the initiation, formation, or continuation of mentoring relationships. They can include organizational behaviors that impede diversified mentoring. Examples include organizational structures that promote segregation by rank, department, or specialization, thereby limiting minority access to relationships; restricted informal and social interactions with minority protégés by majority mentors, thereby making the mentors less comfortable interacting with minority than with majority protégés; the mentor's desire to identify with the protégé as a younger version of himself or herself; and the risk of negative exposure associated with mentoring a minority protégé. When these trends emerge, the negative effects of diversity—of perceived differences among the workforce—also emerge.

While potential barriers that can hinder the effectiveness of mentoring programs do exist, mentoring is a useful strategy. It requires adjustments and synchronization at cultural, structural, and behavioral levels in order to operate effectively.[5]

Unfortunately, contemporary organizations can no longer afford to narrowly view mentoring as only a role reserved for sages who sponsor new recruits or as a tool to deal with diversity issues. Mentoring must become the requirement of every leader in successful organizations. Managers acting as mentors to subordinates raises a special challenge. How does a subordinate comfortably pursue necessary trial and error in front of the person who will ultimately pass judgment on salary increases, promotions, and work assignments? Since learning requires experimentation and risk taking, how does a manager differentiate between an insight goal (such as creativity and discovery) and an in-charge role (command and control)? Power retards learning, so managers as mentors must demonstrate four qualities critical to leveling the learning field. They must be:

> *Purposeful.* They must always take time to communicate the organization's vision and values. Associates should never be confused as to why they are learning a particular skill or receiving cross-training in different areas.

> *Humble.* Humility entails relinquishing efforts to control the outcome. It suggests putting great effort into being authentic and mask-free. It implies a manager is devoted to learning, not just devoted to convincing. Humility is one of the most difficult and courageous interpersonal acts a leader can take with a subordinate. It is also the most powerful.

Curious. There are many by-products of curiosity. Most foster learning. Curious leaders ask a lot of pointed, get-behind-the-issue questions. Curious leaders are interested in people and consequently reach out in ways that are inclusive and show honest interest and positive regard for others.

Generous. Generosity means bestowing value upon another without expectation of reciprocity. A mentor's primary gift is advice conveyed with passion for learning and concern for the learner. Such a gift exemplifies the core of the mentoring role. Advice-giving works only if the context is learning. Begin giving advice by letting the employee know the focus of your mentoring. Make sure you have a "meeting of the minds" in focus. Ask permission to give advice. Avoid phrases such as "you ought to." Keep advice in the first person singular.[6] See figure 2-1.

FIGURE 2-1
Ten Tips for Being a Master Mentor

1. Be willing to confidently reveal your own challenges and frustrations to your protégé.

2. Remove the mask of position as you demonstrate enthusiasm for learning.

3. Display enthusiastic inclusion and curiosity.

4. Avoid "why" questions.

5. Ask questions that make your protégé think—questions that ask for comparison, evaluation, and reflection.

6. Listen.

7. Do not rely on power symbols—sitting behind an imposing desk, for example.

8. Support without rescuing.

9. Be a role model.

10. When it is time for your protégé to move on, celebrate and affirm.

Missions of Mentorship

Many African American children are underexposed to career options such as librarianship. African American librarians must take responsibility for exposing our young people to career options in the library profession. It is understandably difficult for them to prepare for a career that they don't even know exists. Some ways in which African American librarians can fulfill the mission of mentors:

- Arrange tours of various types of libraries for pupils at a local school.
- Recruit at least one college student for an internship at your library.
- Let a young person "shadow" you as you go through your workday.
- Sponsor student memberships in your professional organization.
- Join or organize a mentorship program for a school in your neighborhood.

The advertising industry echoes sentiments very similar to those heard in the library profession. A Black senior executive of a New York agency states: "The larger issue is the racism that exists throughout the industry and the unwillingness to recruit and train African Americans." Some industry insiders are finally admitting that racism and apathy—not a lack of minority talent—are the causes of the industry's lack of diversification. According to the U.S. Bureau of Labor Statistics, African Americans make up 10.1 percent of the nation's workforce, but only 2.1 percent of managers in marketing and public relations and advertising positions.

A survey of 2,500 agency media employees by the trade publication *Mediaweek* in May 1992 showed that less than 1 percent of all workers are Black, and about 2 percent are Hispanic. The advertising industry has rarely kept any focus on minority hiring. From the industry's infancy in the early part of the century until the late 1960s, it was a WASP-dominated profession in which white male captains of industry handed over accounts to the white males controlling the images of the marketplace.

With America's changing demographics, the ad industry's major trade associations, the American Association of Advertising Agencies and the American Advertising Federation (AAF), have decided to step up their efforts to increase the ranks of minorities in the advertising field. The AAF, consisting of 50,000 members, is recruiting minorities to join its professional ad clubs and two hundred college chapters. Members are trying to get into the schools, beginning as low as junior high, to talk about advertising as an active and lucrative field. The association runs the Minority Advertising Intern program, which has offered summer employment to about 650 participants since its inception in 1973.[7]

Mentoring Programs in the Teaching Profession

The teaching profession has long recognized the importance of minority teachers because they (a) serve as role models, (b) may be better able to meet the learning needs of minority students, and (c) are often bilingual and can help students transcend language barriers. Since 1976, the proportion of minority students in public school classrooms has been climbing steadily. The minority teacher population, however, has remained static at around 10 percent.[8] A study by the state of Wisconsin projected that by the year 2000 minority teachers will constitute about 3 percent of its teacher ranks, while the minority student population will be about 38 percent. With the limited number of minority teachers employed in the nation's schools, it is possible for a student to complete high school without ever having had a teacher from a minority group.

Drawing a similar conclusion, the same can be said of libraries in some communities. According to one educator, "it is virtually impossible to truly educate a multicultural population with a homogeneous teaching force." To this end, the teaching profession has established a wide variety of programs to recruit and retain minorities. Research has shown that one universal component of these programs is some type of mentoring.

Electronic Mentoring

MentorNet

MentorNet is the National Electronic Industrial Mentoring Network for Women in Engineering and Science. The network pairs women who are studying engineering or science at a participating university with professional scientists and engineers working in industry and helps them form e-mail-based mentoring relationships.

This organization states that e-mail is convenient, cost-effective, and easy to use. E-mail is also widely available. Using e-mail allows MentorNet program participants to transcend constraints of geography, time, and synchronous communication (that is, there is no need for both parties to be available simultaneously; they can add to the conversation at their convenience). An "e-mentoring" program allows participation of many professionals whose time schedules and constraints prevent them from participating in more traditional relationships with students. Women students from participating universities and mentors sign up for the program using an online application form. Information from the application enters a central database, and sorting software identifies several probable matches. The network's mentoring specialist reviews and completes the match and launches the pair on their e-mail relationship. The mentoring specialist sends out regular electronic newsletters with suggestions for student/mentor pairs and is available to coach and assist participants who encounter difficulties.

Electronic Mentoring and Academic Guidance Network (EMAGN)

This pilot Electronic Mentoring project was launched in 1996 and targets eleventh-grade students at a high school in San Francisco. The program is offered through electronic communication using e-mail, electronic chat rooms, and video conferencing, and it offers a one-on-one relationship with business school undergraduate student volunteers who encourage youth to achieve academic goals and pursue higher educations.

Mentors help students identify college interests and goals and assist them in the decision-making process and the steps required to pursue higher education. The program is designed to help ensure broader access to educational opportunities through the use of communications technology, and it attempts to create a model that eliminates geographical constraints. The project familiarizes youth with interactive technology devices, encourages them to locate college and scholarship information on the World Wide Web, and enables student mentors to communicate more frequently by reducing the frustrations of phone tag, lost messages, and conflicting schedules. The project's goal is to offer a program to increase the number of disadvantaged students who, with support from undergraduate business students, are able to obtain information and mentoring that will enable them to enroll and successfully compete at any university or college.

Hewlett-Packard E-Mail Mentoring Program

The Hewlett-Packard E-Mail Mentoring Program creates one-on-one mentor relationships between its employees and students and teachers from grades five through twelve. HP employees motivate students to excel in math and science and to improve their communication and problem-solving skills. In addition, HP employees help students develop the skills they need to pursue their interests in a professional and successful way.

Mentoring in the Library Profession

Research indicates that there have been several initiatives taken over the years to establish mentoring programs primarily at various academic institutions, but these programs have been the exception rather than the rule. To make a significant impact, the authors believe that a mentoring initiative should come from the national professional organization and perhaps at state levels as well. State library associations could spearhead statewide mentoring initiatives and meet as a unit at the national conferences for information sharing and workshops to provide support for their individual efforts.

The mentor program at UCLA's Graduate School of Education and Information Studies (GSEIS) paired information professionals with first-year library students in a mentor-student relationship. A core of UCLA librarians was joined by librarians from all over southern California. They were recruited from GSEIS alumni, the Southern California Special Libraries Association membership, the Los Angeles Public Library librarians (both adult and children's), and from volunteers who heard of the program and wanted to be involved. The program offers a wide variety of mentors from academic, business, law, medical, museum, public, school, and special libraries.[9]

Another initiative was started by the libraries in the state of Colorado by the Colorado Council on Library Development (CCLD). A statewide committee was formed, which included librarians and laypeople representing the various minority groups as well as representatives from every part of Colorado. The committee's original charge was to develop a statewide plan for addressing library services for "demographically diverse populations." This charge was further refined to focus on the visible minority populations—African American, Asian American, Latino, and Native American. One of the areas of emphasis identified by the committee was personnel training. It was stated that one way to serve minority communities better was to hire minority staff who not only can relate to and understand diverse cultures but also can serve as role models to attract nonusers. A subcommittee designed a mentoring program for the retention and advancement of minority librarians and paraprofessionals, with at least four mentoring teams operating the first year. The mentoring program was designed for seasoned minority or white librarians/mentors to share their knowledge and experiences with minority protégés who could benefit from their guidance and wisdom. The response from both mentors and protégés has been favorable.[10]

Changing Minds Always a Challenge

Lack of money, career gridlock, cultural differences, and personal inclination all contribute to the problem, but many librarians—most minorities, as well as some white librarians—are quick to point out that they feel most in the library profession are often simply inhospitable to those who are different. Minorities still struggle to make inroads in a historically inhospitable profession that has proven resistant to change.

NOTES

1. Steve Hanamura, "Working with People Who Are Different," *Training & Development Journal* 43, no. 6 (June 1989): 11.
2. Ibid., 112-14.
3. Shimon-Craig Van Collie, "Moving Up through Mentoring," *Workforce* 77 (March 1998): 36.
4. Ibid., 40.
5. Deloris McGee Wanguri, "Diversity, Perceptions of Equity, and Communicative Openness in the Workplace," *Journal of Business Communication* 33, no. 4 (Special issue: Diversity in the Workplace) (Oct. 1996): 443.
6. Chip R. Bell, "A New Key to Employee Loyalty: Portable Wisdom (Mentors in a Corporate Environment)," *Management Review* 85, no. 12 (Dec. 1996): 20.
7. Brian Wright O'Connor, "Are Advertising Agencies Serious about Hiring African Americans?" *Black Enterprise* 23 (March 1993): 88.
8. Mary Piercynski, Myrna Matranga, and Gary Peltier, "Legislative Appropriation for Minority Teacher Recruitment: Did It Really Matter?" *The Clearing House* 70 (March-April 1997): 205.
9. Joan Kaplowitz, "Mentoring Library School Students—A Survey," *Special Libraries* 83, no. 4 (fall 1992): 219.
10. Camila A. Alire, "Ethnic Populations: A Model for Statewide Service," *American Libraries* 28, no. 10 (Nov. 1997): 38.

3

Target-Marketing
the Profession

Marketing the career opportunities and importance of libraries in minority communities must become a major issue for library professionals across the country. While minorities make up only 25 percent of the U.S. population, they will contribute 70 percent of growth during this decade. Hispanics will account for 33 percent of the growth; Asian Americans, 20 percent; and African Americans, 17 percent.

Libraries must begin to market their services in a variety of ways, including the use of library professionals who speak a second language and the design of library services targeted to specific ethnic minority markets.

Reaching and serving a racially and ethnically diverse population should be a top priority within the library and information science business for many reasons including numbers: minority groups in the United States are growing six times faster than the non-minority population.

To be successful in effectively introducing the library and information profession to the minority population, we as library professionals must assume the role of public relations practitioners. We need to find ways in which to tailor our services to our nation's ethnic minority population. As public relations practitioners, we must promote the library profession to the many minority markets.

We also must segment these minority audiences if we are to establish and maintain mutually beneficial relationships with all minority groups. In promoting the profession we must not fail to distinguish the important differences among and within minority populations. We must overcome five myths to effectively target our ethnic minority communities:

1. Minorities are the same as Caucasians.

2. Minorities are homogeneous.
3. Libraries and library professionals can effectively utilize mass media to reach all minority populations.
4. Language isn't important.
5. Minorities are interested only in certain careers and services.

We should be very conscious of minorities' differing preferences, which will enhance opportunities to successfully promote the library profession and services. This consciousness will also keep us from offending ethnic minority populations or from overlooking important minority segments of the public altogether.

It is essential that we utilize our pool of talented ethnic minority library professionals to lead the charge in introducing the profession and services to the many ethnic minorities. Many principles to guide a public relations campaign within the African American community concerning our profession and services can apply as well to Asian and Hispanic communities. As mentioned above, we must be sure to address the distinguishing differences among the minority groups. Always provide them with relevant information regarding the library profession and services. Be sure to recognize ethnic minorities by portraying them in non-stereotypical ways and show respect for their culture and values. Recognize them as an asset to the profession. In other words, take the time to study those you wish to recruit to provide library service. The following are just a few distinguishing characteristics that might be useful for you to know in your campaign to successfully reach our minority populations. We are not in a position to speak for all ethnic minority groups, and only feel comfortable providing brief comments regarding the following minority groups. We suggest that library professionals involved in the recruitment process take the time to conduct thorough research on the cultures and backgrounds of the minority groups you plan to recruit to the profession to provide library services.

African Americans

African Americans number almost 30 million and account for more than 12 percent of the U.S. population and 14 percent of its workforce. As we organize a successful strategy to recruit ethnic minorities to the library profession, the African American public must be seriously evaluated.

The library profession can attract the interests of the African American public by providing relevant information about the profession through communications that are linked with certain causes and interests of African Americans. For example, if we decide to introduce the profession through flyers, press releases, and so on, it is important to connect this material to African American interests such as the United Negro College Fund and the Sickle Cell Disease Foundation. We should sponsor special events in correlation with events of popularity within the African American community. Events surrounding African American history or the birth dates of famous African American leaders can be opportune times to promote the profession and services.

We must clearly understand, respect, and accept the fact that many African American values differ from those of Caucasians, and we must address them as such. Showing respect for African American values includes recognizing their attitudes about family, religion, and self-image.

We can increase communication effectiveness if we recognize these values when promoting library and information science to African Americans. The use of photography to promote the library profession to African Americans should portray their sense of style and personal elegance. We can increase message relevance for African Americans by including various products and services as props in visual communications and by referring to them in verbal communications.

Successfully targeting African Americans also demands that library professionals recognize differences between African Americans. They differ by socioeconomic class. Poor African Americans mostly live in the poor inner cities. Wealthier African Americans live in the suburbs, own homes, and are frequently well-educated professionals. Most (53 percent) still live in the South, where they earn low incomes. However, 75 percent are above the poverty level, and 13 percent have annual incomes of $50,000 or more.

Communicating with African Americans in different socioeconomic classes requires different verbal and visual messages. Those in lower socioeconomic classes are most likely to respond to visual and verbal messages that appeal to their desire to improve their position. They are the ones who usually take a direct hit from the burdens of injustice delivered by whites within our racist society. However, middle-class African Americans are able to adjust and handle the burden of racism and ongoing prejudice in a different manner. When necessary, they can blend African American culture with middle-class American lifestyles. Independent and self-confident, middle-class African Americans don't feel a need to impress anyone, especially Caucasians. And they must be treated accordingly.

We must attract more African Americans to the profession to effectively deliver the message of career opportunities in library and information science. Also, as mentioned throughout this book, attracting more African Americans to the profession will enhance the manner in which the library profession and services are perceived and received by the African American community.

Screening in the Barbershop

The medical staff at Southwest hospital located in Washington, D.C., consistently attempted to find new and more effective ways in which to provide health services to the African American community. The staff had organized a wellness program specifically designed to address the medical needs of members of their urban poor African American community. In one particular program, the hospital needed to attract African American males to the hospital to be screened for hypertension, which has been a serious medical concern for the African American community for quite some time. The hospital advertised the day of the screening through press releases, public service announcements, flyers, and even commercial spots on television. The day of the screening hospital representatives were astounded by the poor response to the program. Very few African American men responded because many of them do not respond to screening promotions of this nature. They resist taking the time out of their schedules to make a trip to the community hospital. In most cases, this kind of appointment is not a top priority within the African American male's schedule. He knows that the screenings are important, but he just cannot seem to get there. The hospital moved the screenings to the community library, a strategy used to take the program out of the medical environment. Here again, African American men did not respond, although the participation was greater at the library.

If your goal is to successfully provide a service or deliver a message to the African American community, you must *go to* and become *involved in* the African American community. You must take the time to learn the culture and lifestyle of the minority population with which you are attempting to make contact.

The hospital hired an African American female, Pamala B. Holmes, to serve as the hospital's Community Service Coordinator (outreach person). Her responsibility was to appeal to the minority community and design and establish medical programs that would directly address the specific medical needs of the African American community. Her first assignment was to resurrect the hypertension screening program, the program that the hospital had unsuccessfully attempted to implement. Pam, familiar with the neighborhood and the culture of the people, began to strategically plan her approach to the hypertension project. To make an involved success story brief, she set the screening program up in the community barbershop—the shop that almost every African American male in the neighborhood visited at least once every two weeks. Every male who visited that barbershop agreed to a screening. It was not long before every customer had taken the time for the screening based simply on the fact that the screenings were made available in a popular and convenient location. The hypertension project became so popular that the owner of the barbershop gained nineteen new customers!

The point is that we must clearly understand the personality of the ethnic minority community before we can successfully launch a marketing plan that attracts the attention of minorities for recruitment or for providing quality library services.

Asian Americans

The 1990 census counted more than seven million Asian Americans for 3.5 percent of the U.S. population. Some researchers claim that the census underrepresented Asian Americans and that ten million more accurately reflects this population. According to some marketers, Asian Americans represent the nation's fastest-growing market.

Much of this growth comes from immigration. Of the 30 percent who moved to the United States since 1970, 75 percent immigrated from 1980 to 1990. Most (69 percent) live in 25 metropolitan areas, with 39 percent living in California.

They are the wealthiest of all minorities, averaging annual incomes of $38,500 in 1995 compared with $31,000 for Caucasians. More than 32 percent of Asian Americans have family incomes exceeding $50,000, compared with only 29 percent of Caucasian families. In 1992, Asian Americans spent $120 billion. Only 11 percent of Asian American families live in poverty.

One reason Asian Americans fare so well economically is that most are married, and both husband and wife work. Almost three-quarters of Asian Americans are employed, with 89 percent of those employed working in white collar jobs. Another reason they fare well economically is that they highly value education, with 74 percent completing college.

Asian Americans share many values that provide guidelines to targeting them as a group. Most (80 percent) are married. They do not believe in divorce, so their divorce rate is low. They have a high respect for older people, and often several generations live together, making for large families.

Asian Americans include many different subgroups—Asian Indian, Chinese, Hawaiian, Japanese, Korean, Philippine, Vietnamese, and others. Providing relevant information about the library profession to Asian Americans requires that we recognize subgroups' differences in language, culture, and demographics.

As library professionals we can reach Asian Americans through news releases more effectively than any other minority group. However, we need to produce news releases and other promotional material in the language of the subgroups and promote the profession in their newspapers. Most (94 percent) read newspapers, with 82 percent reading newspapers in their native languages.

We can also reach Asian Americans through their television programs and subcarrier radio channels. Japanese and Indians own five television companies that produce programming in New York City. The Pacific Century, a PBS program, reaches Asian Americans. Sinocast Radio, a national broadcast, reaches Chinese.

We can also effectively reach Asian Americans through events and community organizations. Supporting such festivals provides the relevant involvement necessary to reach any minority group.[1]

Hispanic Americans

The Hispanic American population is predicted to grow to 30 million by the year 2000 and 41.2 million by 2020. This population is about 75 percent (13 million) Mexicans, who live mostly in southwestern and western states, with the remaining 25 percent Cubans (1 million), who live mainly in Florida; Puerto Ricans (2.5 million) who live mainly in New York, New Jersey, and Chicago; and others (2.2 million) who primarily come from Central and South America. In 1990, Hispanics lived primarily in California, Texas, New York, Florida, and Illinois. Some members of the Hispanic community live in intergenerational families that include children, parents, and grandparents.

Hispanic Americans as a group share several characteristics. Two of the most important are language and religion. Although many are bilingual, most speak only Spanish. Library professionals will have little success communicating with Hispanic Americans through the mass media. Less than 10 percent use mass media, and only 50 percent read English. Minority newspapers such as *La Opinion* and radio and television stations such as Telemundo reach many, but direct mail in Spanish reaches them better.

Although Protestantism is the fastest growing religion among Hispanics, most are Catholics. They value family, children, traditional middle-class values, aesthetics, emotions, and appearance. Using recruitment strategies or techniques that center around Hispanic values provides relevance and increases the effectiveness of your recruitment or service efforts.

Hispanic Americans work hard to maintain their ethnicity, including observing holidays, rituals, and festivals. Sponsoring or participating in these events demonstrates support for and builds relationships with Hispanic Americans. Major events occur annually in Miami; New York; Washington, D.C.; Chicago; Houston; San Francisco; and Brownsville, Texas. The top three—Calle Ocho in Miami and the Puerto Rican Day and Hispanic Day parades in New York—each reach more than a million Hispanic Americans annually.

Each segment of the Hispanic American population deserves individual attention. Library professionals should understand that a target-specific approach to various segments of the Hispanic American population is extremely important. They may differ by country of origin, culture, beliefs, and opinions.[2]

Native Americans

It is so extremely important that everyone, especially our young people, construct positive images of present-day Native American people to prevent racial or cultural stereotypes from becoming part of their beliefs. American Indian people are among the many different peoples and cultures that live on the American continent. While we all are much more alike than different, it is the differences that too often compel us to erect barriers of misunderstanding. Consequently, we must learn more about each other. Understanding more about the Native American community will enable library professionals to effectively market the profession and provide quality library service to the community.

- We should be aware that Native American people prefer to be identified by their nation's name (for example, Navajo, Menominee, Seneca). The name "Indian" was a white man's invention and still remains largely a white image, if not a stereotype.

- Most Native American people prefer to be recognized as belonging to a particular nation of people rather than a tribe. While "tribe" or "tribal society" may be acceptable to some Native American people, others believe the words suggest primitive or nomadic peoples—a classification most modern populations find offensive. A nation, on the other hand, is defined as having political organization and its own administrative structure.

- We must be sensitive to and find ways to distinguish cultural variations when working with people from different nations.

- Native Americans are often used as icons on commercial products ranging from foods and automobiles to athletic teams. We must clearly understand that representations of the bow and arrow, tomahawks, war bonnets, feathers, and war paint are depictions of a mythical Native American from a long-gone era. Native people have changed over the centuries as have the many American immigrants who came later.[3]

Conclusion

The many groups and subgroups of American minorities require that library professionals interested in successfully promoting the profession must use techniques that marketers and advertisers have already begun to use. If we are to truly address the issue of recruitment and providing quality library services to the ethnic minority populations of this country, all things must be considered:

- Cater messages to the different tastes of each group or subgroup.
- Communicate in each group's native tongue. (This is especially important for Hispanic and Asian Americans.)
- Promote recruitment to the profession through the use of ethnic minority library professionals who can be very instrumental in targeting their own particular minority group.
- Make promotional and campaign decisions based on careful research information concluded from demographic information.

The proactive recruitment of minority groups into the library science profession has been minimal. This is despite the prediction that four cultural minority groups (African, Hispanic, Asian, and Native Americans) will soon form one-third of the U.S. population. The American Library Association has provided little support to effect changes until very recently, with the introduction of the Spectrum Initiative. It is time for ALA to engage in the direct sponsorship of a marketing strategy that will ensure the recruitment of minority librarians so that quality library services reach a broader spectrum of Americans. The library profession is losing ground in recruiting ethnic minorities to the profession, while the ethnic makeup of the nation increases.

There are many theories on why African, Hispanic, Asian, and Native Americans have had little or no opportunity to become involved in library and information science. Many of them mirror societal ills such as racism and prejudice. Others reflect educational and financial barriers. It is our opinion that these ethnic groups have not traditionally looked to library and information science as a glamorous career option, while others contend that they have been generally overlooked by the profession for many, many years. Affirmative action policies have been slightly instrumental in increasing minority representation in the library and information science profession, but we as library administrators must take an active role in marketing the library profession in such a way that it attracts the attention of our minority populations.

We must develop a strategic plan of recruitment with objectives and activities that will include marketing the profession in such a manner that it piques the interests of our minority population, beginning with our minority youth population (junior and senior high school students) through undergraduate and graduate level students. We as library professionals must aggressively promote the promising career opportunities available in a career in library and information science.

Minority talent is there, but minorities need to be made aware of the career potential of library and information science. The profession has a reason, beyond legal and moral responsibility, as it relates to the changing demographics of society. Minorities must be informed that there is something within this profession to offer them.

Making ethnic minorities aware of opportunities in library and information science involves more than traveling to college campuses or placing ads. The recruitment strategy must include aligning with minority-affiliated organizations. What the library profession fails to realize is that when you are looking for minority recruits, you have a special situation on your hands. In many cases, you must go down non-traditional paths to find interested or potential candidates. You could possibly find a good number of white employees by placing ads in newspapers in mostly white communities or online, but if you are sincere in your effort to recruit minorities, your recruitment strategy must include aligning with minority-affiliated organizations. Seek professional library organizations to assist with networking and promoting the profession, including the ethnic caucuses of the American Library Association. Use the assistance of minority alumni to identify potential minority students.

We also must change how we advertise and promote our profession to the ethnic minority media. Many ads ask the wrong questions, for example: "Have you thought about librarianship as a career?" Well, the answer is usually no. The question should be changed to sound more appealing and to emphasize personal qualities—analytical thinking, independence—and then the response may be positive. For example:

> If you enjoy books and like working with people and computers, check out a career as a Librarian/Information Specialist. It could be one of your best decisions ever! If you're resourceful, enterprising, and creative, you'll enjoy the challenge of being a Librarian/Information Specialist. For additional information, contact your local library or librarian or visit the Web page of the American Library Association.

Many cite college campuses, career fairs, and community employment agencies, including the Internet, as sources for potential candidates. Companies tend to go to Yale University and similar schools, but if they do not see Black students, they automatically think that Blacks are not interested and don't seek them out as a result. Unless this profession takes the initiative to aggressively market and recruit, this profession is going to stay primarily homogeneous.

We as library professionals need to promote the fact that there are many career options beyond the traditional library service. Jobs are available in the publishing and information industries and in many other industries that need the information management skills developed in library education.

The library industry's ability to serve the growing market of minority representation may be adversely affected by its failure to attract more African, Asian, Hispanic, and Native American employees into the profession. The recruitment of minorities to the library profession means being competitive and keeping your edge. When individuals from varied ethnic backgrounds become actively involved in the library profession, they will certainly bring a different set of eyes and ears to the table that will enhance the way in which we do business. We must approach library and information science as a business. A successful marketing strategy will gain the attention of our minority population. It is not enough to simply say it's the right thing to do.

Introducing the library profession as a truly viable career option for people of color is a second initiative the American Library Association should undertake in an effort to attract more ethnic minorities to the profession. Too few members of the ethnic minority population know about the vast opportunities available when pursuing a career in library and information science. As with the Spectrum Initiative, ALA must invest the necessary time and make the required effort to prepare an effective marketing plan designed to introduce the library profession to this targeted audience. A marketing plan would provide an arranged structure to guide the process of determining the audience and detailing the needs and wants of this targeted audience. We would then be in a position to establish a relationship with ethnic minority communities and identify the most effective ways in which to introduce our profession. Members of the ethnic minority population must be convinced that choosing a career in library and information science is a very challenging and beneficial career option.

Today individuals have more career choices than ever before, and they also have more information about the choices. It is important that ALA understands that target-marketing drives not only our marketing decisions but also our recruitment strategies and the entire decision-making framework as it pertains to this issue.

Publicity can play a unique role as a tool in the marketing plan. It is especially valuable in a wide range of situations in which public awareness or public opinion is critical to your marketing success. Educating the target audience and countering misconceptions about the profession can be accomplished through quality publicity. Publicity is media communication that helps build target market awareness and positively affects attitudes toward whatever is being promoted. In a publicity program, the American Library Association could provide information used to promote the profession to the national news media. Publicity provides the means to tell your story in greater depth and in a manner that tends to be informational rather than promotional. A long-term investment in publicity can be a tremendous asset when you need to educate and build awareness and understanding of the library profession. Positive publicity is the result of a written, well-thought-out plan with well-defined objectives and strategies. We must ensure that the publicity we disseminate creates positive awareness of the profession. Think carefully about the information available to release and how we can enhance its presentation. Several types of articles and stories will generate publicity: a standard news release, feature stories, concept articles, photo opportunities, and public service announcements.

Merchandising is another marketing strategy that can be used to make a visual or written statement about the library profession. Merchandising includes brochures, sell sheets, product displays, video presentations, banners, posters, table tents, or any other vehicles that can be used to communicate. These materials should be distributed and located in areas that are popular with the ethnic minority public.

Designing a Quality Recruitment Video

Designing a quality recruitment video is a merchandising strategy that grabs the attention of almost everyone. It must be a well-produced recruitment video designed to attract the attention of the targeted audience. The video must feature ethnic minorities serving in significant roles within the profession. With over 120 million VCRs in homes, schools, and businesses across the United States, thousands of companies have found that video is a powerful way to market goods, services, and ideas. The creation of a quality video designed to recruit minorities to the library profession is essential to the overall recruitment process. Brochures are also needed, but brochures do not convey action, music, and drama the way a video does. The video is an excellent marketing tool that can play an essential role in the recruitment of ethnic minorities of all ages and backgrounds to the library and information science profession. The American Library Association has produced recruitment videos in the past, but with little or no participation by ethnic minorities. It is time for an updated recruitment video that is suitable for all those viewing and that also features ethnic minorities serving in key positions within the profession.

A quality video production is expensive; even a ten-minute, no-frills production will cost at least $10,000 to $20,000. Conventional wisdom says if you cannot spend a minimum of $15,000, don't even consider video as a promotional or recruitment tool. The video must achieve your business goal.

Proposal (Funding)

The creation of a high quality recruitment video is a costly endeavor. The approximate current rate for the production of a high quality video is $3,000 per minute. A ten-minute video will cost the client $30,000, a substantial cut into your library budget. Alternative funding may be the only way in which you can obtain the needed dollars to have a video of high quality produced. There may be a need to write a recruitment video proposal that you can submit to your state and local library organizations. The following is an example of a format that can be used in securing needed funding for your recruitment video. A similar format was successful in the state of Ohio, and we hope it will assist you in securing needed funding.

PROPOSAL

The Public Library of Newbury proposes development of an 8- to 10-minute video designed to recruit middle and high school students to the library profession, with an emphasis on the recruitment of minorities. A special task force of library professionals will direct the content focus of the video; production will be done by a commercial firm under contract to the Public Library of Newbury.

One copy of the video will be distributed to each of the public library systems within the state, and copies will be sent to guidance counselors at selected high schools. Additional copies will be made available for sale.

The Public Library of Newbury will develop a packet of materials to accompany the video and will work on additional efforts to enhance the recruitment of minorities to the library profession.

Background

Since 1992, the Public Library of Newbury has had a committee designed to recommend ways in which the Public Library of Newbury can address the need for the recruitment and retention of minorities in librarianship within the state. In pursuit of this goal, the committee has the following objectives:

1. To heighten awareness throughout the state of the need for a diverse professional workforce in the field of librarianship.

2. To coordinate a program on staff diversity in libraries at our annual conference.

3. To recommend direction and activities to the Public Library of Newbury's board of trustees for continuing progress and commitment in the area of diversity.

One of the long-held beliefs of this committee is the need to educate students at the junior high and high school levels about careers in libraries. The recommended vehicle for accomplishing this is a brief video. Such a video could be used at career days, by students individually in their school or public library, and by guidance counselors working with students in classes or on a one-to-one basis.

Target-Marketing the Profession

Program

The Public Library of Newbury recruitment committee will meet on July 25-26 to develop goals for the video. At this meeting, the committee will make final decisions regarding:

- the target audience
- content focus of the video
- methods of distribution
- additional materials and programs to be developed in support of the video and recruitment effort

Following this session, we will contract with a video production company to produce the video. We will identify two or three different production companies and seek bids based on the report of the committee. Following acceptance of a bid, members of the committee will meet with the producer/director regarding specifics of the production.

Production will begin in August and be completed by mid-September. Editing and duplication of copies will be done in late September, and the video will be available for distribution in early October.

Production of accompanying print materials may not be completed by this date; however, we do hope to introduce the video at the state annual conference in late October.

Project Management

The Public Library of Newbury will serve as fiscal agent for this project. Ms. Victoria Dennis, Executive Director, will be the project manager. Our committee will develop the content focus of the video. Video production will be contracted to a video producer via a bid process.

Members of the committee will develop the ancillary materials to accompany the video. The State Library will publish all print materials and will handle distribution of the video. A list of committee members and their library affiliations is attached.

Dr. Tom Jones, Dean of our School of Library and Information Science, will serve as an ad hoc member of the committee during the development and production of the video.

Video Distribution

We will duplicate large numbers of the video once completed to get the volume discount. A distribution plan must be designed. It is not enough just to produce a great recruitment video; the video must reach its target audience.

Because the purpose of the video is to recruit middle and high school students to the library profession with an emphasis on the recruitment of minorities, we will distribute copies to each public library system in the state and to high school guidance counselors in selected high schools. As additional copies of the video are sold, we will use the funds from the sales to produce additional videos for distribution to schools.

The Public Library of Newbury Recruitment Committee

Victoria Dennis, Chair
Executive Director, The Public Library of Newbury

Robert Webb, Trustee
The Public Library of Newbury

Hattie Mattering, Librarian
University of Newbury

Parker Ethington, Deputy Director
Carterstown Public Library

Nancy Washington
The State Library

Edward Smalls, Branch Manager
Carterstown Public Library

Deidra Sharpton, Librarian
Newbury Metropolitan Hospital

James Thorton, Corporate Vice President
Dynasty Industries

Dr. Tom Jones, Dean
School of Library and Information Science

Production Company

Locate a quality video production company and let these experts guide your production with a librarian(s) serving as consultant or client producer throughout the process. The ultimate goal is to produce a quality recruitment video that creates a specific response among targeted viewers.

The first steps in planning a successful recruitment video are scripting, shooting, and editing. A great marketing video must be designed to attract and hold the viewer's attention. If this is not achieved, the entire production is a waste of money and time.

The sound track of the video is often the music and dialogue that allows the scenes of the production to flow smoothly into one entity. It also often transcends the impact of the visual elements, leading the viewer to experience the video on an emotional level. Different types of music can dramatically change the mood or impact of the production. Music helps drive the visuals and make the video more compelling.

The script is a blueprint for both the shooting and editing of a video. The script brings order to a complex process full of details. There are six questions to answer before writing the script for a successful recruitment video:

1. Who is the targeted audience?
2. In what setting will they watch?
3. What is the goal or objective of the video?
4. Will printed materials accompany the video?
5. How will the video be distributed?
6. Will the video need to be regularly updated?

Remember the Audience

Your intended audience is everything. The people of the audience are your reason for making this recruitment video. Their reaction to the video determines whether it's successful. If you make this video to please only yourself, you are making at best an art film, at worst a home movie. Producing a short recruitment video is more effective than a long production. Remember, this is not entertainment like a sitcom, feature film, or talk show. Audiences pay for those entertainments whether they buy a movie ticket or watch hundreds of little advertisements called commercials. Your audience is much less motivated and will not tolerate a long and boring video production.[4]

Release Form Needed
for Those Who Participate

There will be a need to produce a release for those who participate in your video production. Figure 3-1 is an example of the type of release form that may be used by you and your production company. This is only an example; there are several approaches to addressing the release information. Please consult your legal counsel to ensure that the appropriate information is included in your release form.

FIGURE 3-1
Release

I, _____, being of legal age and intending to be legally bound, do hereby consent and otherwise give permission to the ABC production group, in consideration of my time, talent, and services; to include me in still photographs, motion picture photography and/or videotape in connection with television commercials and/or promotions being produced, and do hereby grant to the ABC production group the perpetual right to use any such still photographs, motion picture photography and/or videotape or the respective negatives, reproductions and/or copies of the original prints and/or negatives along with any sound track recording contemporaneously or subsequently produced. I further consent to and grant the ABC production group the right, license, and privilege to substitute the voice and/or sound effects of other persons for my voice and/or sound track recording made in conjunction with or subsequent to the aforementioned still photographs, motion picture photography, or videotape. I further consent to and grant the ABC production group the right to change, substitute, or alter my name or likeness in connection with the use, exhibition, advertising, exploitation, or any other commercial or non-profit use of the aforementioned still photographs, motion picture photography, and/or videotape together with the sound track recording of my voice and do further consent and give permission to the ABC production group to use, distribute, sell, assign, and otherwise retain the aforementioned photographs, motion picture photography, and/or videotape along with any sound track recording made contemporaneously or subsequently thereto.

WITNESS: _____

_____
SIGNATURE

_____
ADDRESS

_____
DATE

DATE: _____ JOB # _____ CLIENT: _____

Thanks for being on our show.

For participants who are under the age of 18, we recommend that the format shown in figure 3-2 be used:

FIGURE 3-2
Release for Minors

Please sign this form, which gives us the permission to use your appearance on our show. We will send you a copy of the show as our thanks for your help. Your signature allows us and our client to use your appearance on this or successive programs. Sorry, no further payments or notifications can be provided.

Thanks again!

ABC production group
1375 Cinema Avenue
Detroit, MI 44115

I agree to appear in your show(s):

Name _____

Address _____

City _____ State _____ Zip _____

Phone _____

Following is the signature of my parent or legal guardian who agrees to the above terms:

_____
PARENT/LEGAL GUARDIAN

_____
NAME/PHONE NUMBER

We suggest that support materials accompany the video. In many cases, information is more appropriate in printed form than in video format.

Brochure for Recruitment Video
(Support Materials)

It is essential that support materials be developed to accompany your recruitment video. The support material can be in the form of brochures that are attractively designed and easy to read and comprehend. The examples that follow are based on a recruitment video, "Me! A Librarian!" produced in the state of Ohio. The video was designed to target young people in junior and senior high school. We hope that these suggestions and recommendations will be helpful as you embark upon your very important video project.

There should be two well-designed brochures to support the video before, during, and after viewing the production.

1. A guide for the instructor, librarian, or whoever is presenting the video to students.

2. A guide for students that provides pertinent information regarding the profession and stimulates a question and answer dialog between the instructor and the viewing audience. An informational piece regarding the profession that students can take home and refer to after the video presentation.

Instructor Video Guide

We recommend that the information within the instructor video guide be structured in the following manner. The brochure should be three-fold and very attractive.

LIBRARY/INFORMATION SPECIALIST

Students who enjoy working with people and using computer technology may be interested in learning more about a career as a Librarian/Information Specialist. The video introduces the exciting and challenging world of Library and Information Science. Individuals actively and successfully working in the profession share their excitement about the profession.

Before Viewing

Find out what students know about librarians, libraries, and information science. Ask them:

- What contact have you had with a Librarian?

- What is an Information Specialist?
- What does a Librarian/Information Specialist do?
- What training is needed to become a Librarian/Information Specialist?

After Viewing

Discuss what a Librarian/Information Specialist does. Compare students' earlier answers.

- Works in many businesses and institutions. (Identify businesses and institutions. Ask students if they can think of other places where a Librarian/Information Specialist might work, for example, school, park service, human resource agency.)
- Helps people find answers to important questions.
- Conducts computer research to locate information for patrons or customers.
- Explains how to use computers and other tools to conduct successful research.
- Helps people find interesting books to read.
- Assists customers who want to "do" something—repair their car, cook a turkey, make a quilt, build a bookcase—by helping them find books with instructions.
- Solves customers' problems by finding information and answers.
- Designs educational and entertaining programs and services.
- Provides services that improve people's lives.

Discuss skills needed by the Librarian/Information Specialist. Compare earlier answers.

- Good communication skills.
- Ability to read and clearly understand written material.
- Good listening skills.
- A four-year college degree in a discipline plus a master's degree in Library and Information Science.

What school subjects might be of benefit to a Librarian/Information Specialist? Courses such as computer science, American and English literature, geography, history, science, art and music, drama, speech, sociology, and psychology. Since a college degree is required, students should position themselves to get such a degree.

What types of jobs are available to the Librarian/Information Specialist?

- Management: administering the library, supervising a department, developing and managing the budget, participating in planning, representing the library in the community.
- Adult services: assisting customers with research; answering questions; selecting and reviewing books, videos, and other library materials; presenting book talks; working with customers with special needs (for example, visually or physically impaired, homebound).
- Young adult and children's services: working with schools, reading stories to young children, planning teen activities, directing summer reading clubs.
- Automation and technical services: specializing in the use of computers to manage information, organizing library materials, developing computer services to help customers and other librarians find information quickly and easily.

Related Projects

For students who are seriously interested in a library/information science career, explore the possibility of shadowing a librarian or schedule a site visit to different types of libraries. Invite a librarian/information specialist to visit school and discuss his or her job responsibilities with the students. Be sure the students prepare questions ahead of time.

Discussion Points

- What are some benefits of entering this profession?
- How do skills needed for this job relate to other jobs?
- What opportunities are there for advancement?

Wages

Find current salaries for librarians/information specialists using information published annually in *American Libraries*, a journal of the American Library Association.[5]

A student guide provided to counselors and other librarians is a good way to get the attention of students. One format is shown in figure 3-3.

FIGURE 3-3

Student Guide

If you enjoy books, like working with people, like computers, and want to know the answers, check out a career as a Librarian/Information Specialist. It could be just the right way to position yourself!

Librarian/Information Specialists

- Work in libraries, schools, colleges, museums, hospitals, law firms, correctional facilities, corporations, government agencies, research laboratories, and religious organizations.
- Perform research to help people find answers to important questions.
- Use computers to locate information for customers.
- Teach customers how to use computers and other research tools.
- Design entertaining and educational programs and services.
- Help patrons select books, videos, compact discs, and tapes they might enjoy.
- Can become supervisors and managers.
- Design, plan, and operate computer systems.

If you're resourceful, enterprising, and creative, you'll enjoy the challenge of being a Librarian/Information Specialist.

What Do You Need?

- Good communication skills including speaking with the public, listening to what people say, reading and understanding written materials.
- Computer skills, especially keyboard skills.
- Courses in high school that will help you get a college degree. Librarians have a four-year college degree in any field (usually liberal arts), plus a master's degree in Library and Information Science.

Start Positioning Yourself!

If you're interested in knowing more about a career as a Librarian/Information Specialist, get some experience in working with the public. Working in a library, fast food restaurant, or retail store is a good first step. The experience will help you position yourself for a challenging, exciting career in Library and Information Science.

(Continued)

FIGURE 3-3 *(Continued)*

Arm yourself with excellent verbal and computer skills. Take time to participate in training to improve your skills. Above all, keep a positive attitude.

Skills you acquire in preparation for becoming a Librarian/Information Specialist can help position you for the future.

Incentives along the Way

The average starting salary for a Librarian/Information Specialist is $25,000 to $30,000. Positions also may offer vacation time and benefits such as health insurance. Like any job, the more experience and education you have, the more money you are likely to be paid.

Librarians/Information Specialists use their talents and skills to provide a very important service—the dissemination of information! If you're resourceful, enterprising, and creative, you'll surely enjoy the challenges associated with a career in Library and Information Science.

Find Out More

Contact a librarian. Ask if you can interview or shadow him or her for an hour or two to observe his or her job. Ask your librarian for further information on careers in Library/Information Science.

SOURCE: State Library of Ohio and Ohio Library Council, "Me! A Librarian!" promotional brochure (1988).

Order Form

Once the video is complete and ready for distribution, there must be an order form designed so that individuals can purchase the video. The order form should include the following:

1. Title of recruitment video.
2. A brief description of the video (for example, "an exciting, 10-minute video designed to interest middle through high school students in a library career. It's fast-paced, informative, and targeted for 13-18 year olds. Appealing to students from all backgrounds!").
3. Include the cost of the video and mention the student and instructor guides that come with the purchase.
4. Include shipping information and payment arrangements.
   Note: The order form should be colorful and visually attractive.

Stop Talking, Start Doing

We can also target-market our minority communities by ensuring that our libraries are tailored to address and fulfill specific library needs of the minority public. Minority library professionals have always been enthusiastic about initiatives that ensure that our libraries and the library profession are sensitive to the needs of our minority population. Colleague Camila A. Alire, Dean of Libraries, Colorado State University, presented the following plan of action while coping with the issue of making library services accessible to our minority public. At the 1996 Stop Talking and Start Doing recruitment workshop, Alire, a dynamic and energetic presenter, delivered a message regarding the state of Colorado's commitment to making both public and academic libraries attractive to the minority public. Alire served as chair of the Colorado Council on Library Development Committee on Library Services to Ethnic Populations (a.k.a. Ethnic Pops Committee). This committee produced a document entitled *Walking the Walk: The Colorado Perspective*. The report has five areas of emphasis that demonstrate the kind of commitment needed to make such initiatives successful.

1. Library Personnel Training
   a. Colorado Libraries will recruit, hire, and retain ethnic minority personnel.
   b. Members of Colorado's ethnic minority populations will be treated by library staff members with sensitivity, courtesy, and respect.

2. Library Services
   Colorado libraries will develop services and programs to meet the information needs of ethnic minorities and to reflect diverse cultural values.

3. Collection Development
   Colorado libraries will contain a wide variety of materials by, about, and in the language of the state's ethnic minority populations.

4. Celebrations
   Colorado libraries will celebrate the heritage and culture of Colorado's ethnic minority populations.

5. Partnerships
   Colorado libraries will develop partnerships with community groups to better serve ethnic minority populations.

This committee also produced a model statement for public libraries that reads as follows:

MODEL STATEMENT FOR PUBLIC LIBRARIES

The _____ Library believes that all people in the community should be encouraged to use the public library and that the library should be prepared to meet their needs. The Library also believes that all people in our community need to understand and appreciate the varying cultures of people who live in Colorado. To that end, the _____ Library endorses the following principles:

1. The _____ Library will recruit, hire, and advance ethnic staff to reflect the ethnic make-up of our community.
2. The _____ Library staff will treat members of ethnic groups with sensitivity, courtesy, and respect.
3. The _____ Library will offer services designed with the ethnic populations in its community in mind.
4. The collection of the _____ Library will contain a wide variety of materials, by, about, and in the language of the state's ethnic populations.
5. The _____ Library will celebrate the heritage and culture of Colorado's ethnic population.
6. The _____ Library will develop partnerships with community groups to better serve ethnic populations.

The document also provides a list of desired outcomes with timelines, for example:

1. By December, 1996, 50 percent of Colorado public and academic libraries will adopt a policy statement on library service to ethnic minority populations.
2. By December, 1996, 30 percent of public and academic libraries and school media centers will conduct a needs assessment of their community's ethnic minorities.
3. By December, 1997, 30 percent of public and academic libraries will develop services that relate to the library's scope and mission.
4. By December, 1996, 70 percent of libraries that have over 3 percent of a targeted ethnic minority population in their service area will offer programming, materials, and services to attract and serve that targeted ethnic minority population.

5. By December, 1996, 70 percent of Colorado libraries' written collection development policies will include a commitment to purchase ethnic and cultural awareness materials and those policies will be implemented.

6. By December, 1996, 70 percent of Colorado libraries will offer cultural awareness materials, programs, exhibits, and/or cultural celebrations to their service populations.

7. By December, 1996, 50 percent of local libraries will establish a working relationship with local ethnic minority and/or other organizations to develop services to ethnic populations.

8. By December, 1999, 50 percent of public libraries that have over 3 percent of a targeted ethnic minority population in their service area will have appropriate ethnic minority representation on their boards of trustees.

9. By December, 1996, 70 percent of Colorado public and academic libraries will adopt recruitment and retention guidelines for ethnic minorities.

10. By December, 1996, 25 percent of libraries that have over 3 percent of a targeted ethnic minority population in their service area will increase their minority professionals.

11. By December, 1996, 30 percent of libraries that have over 3 percent of a targeted ethnic minority population in their service area will increase their minority paraprofessionals.

The commitment to improving library service to ethnic minority communities must be demonstrated in ways very similar to *Walking the Walk: The Colorado Perspective*. Each state must sincerely commit to providing quality library service to ethnic minority communities. The American Library Association can work in cooperation with local ethnic minority library organizations in designing initiatives that will enhance the quality of library service to ethnic minority communities. What are you doing in your state?

The American Library Association, along with state and local library organizations, should put forth an effort to use these and other marketing strategies to assist with the recruitment of people of color to the profession and improve the quality of library service in ethnic minority communities.

A successful target marketing strategy needs the support of library professionals across the country.

NOTES

1. Linda P. Morton, "Targeting Minority Publics," *Public Relations Quarterly* 42, no. 2 (summer 1997): 23.
2. Ibid.
3. Gerry D. Haukoos and Archie B. Beauvais, "Creating Positive Cultural Images," *Childhood Education* 73, no. 2 (winter 1996): 77.
4. Hal Landen, *Marketing with Video* (New York: Oaktree Press, 1996).
5. State Library of Ohio and Ohio Library Council, "Me! A Librarian!" Promotional Brochure (1988).

4

Recruitment at the Junior and Senior High School Levels

By the year 2010, as many as 38 percent of Americans under the age of eighteen will belong to minority groups. In seven states and the District of Columbia, more than half of children will be minorities. In an additional nineteen states, at least one-quarter of children will be Black, Hispanic, Asian, or other minorities.

These statistics, gleaned from several U.S. Census Bureau projections and *American Demographics'* estimates, reveal that dramatic changes are in store as a diverse new generation of Americans replaces older generations dominated by whites. School districts in the nation's largest states will have to adjust to a student body that is more diverse than ever. Businesses that market to children will have to adapt to a rainbow coalition of parents who are proud of their ancestry but anxious to see their children succeed in mainstream America.[1]

Overall, 20 percent of American children will be racial minorities—primarily Black or Asian American—during the 1990s, according to the Census Bureau. By 2000, that share will grow to 21 percent of the population under age 18, and to 23 percent by 2010.

When the white Hispanic population under age eighteen is joined with Blacks and Asians, the minority youth population will grow from 20 percent to 31 percent of the total youth population during the 1990s, from 21 percent to 34 percent in the 2000s, and from 23 percent to 38 percent in 2010.

By 2010, 80 percent of children in Hawaii will be non-white or Hispanic. Minorities will also form the majority of children in New Mexico (77 percent), California (57 percent), Texas (57 percent), New York (53 percent), Florida (53 percent), and Louisiana (50 percent). In the District of Columbia, 93 percent of children will be minorities by 2010.[2]

Where the Kids Are

New York leads the 50 states in the growth of the minority share of its youth population, rising from 40 percent to 53 percent from 1990 to 2010. California follows with an increase of 11 percentage points. Third is Texas with a rise of 10 percentage points, followed by New Mexico (9.5 percentage points) and New Jersey and Illinois (a 9 percentage point increase in each state).

The total youth population of all races and ethnicities combined will grow fastest in the Sunbelt and in states that receive large numbers of immigrants. The only notable exceptions are New Hampshire and Utah. Between 1990 and 2010, the ten states with the fastest-growing youth populations will be New Mexico (up 22 percent); Arizona (21 percent); Alaska (18 percent); Georgia and Florida (17 percent each); California, Nevada, and New Hampshire (12 percent each); and Utah (10 percent).[3]

In the last two decades, businesses watched the mass market explode into hundreds of demographic, lifestyle, and geographic segments. Over the next 20 years, children will lead the way toward an even more diverse future. Fast-food companies, toy manufacturers, and others that depend on the young will need to scrutinize these trends and their strategic implications. Public schools, especially, will have to meet the educational needs of increasingly diverse students. The states and local areas most blessed with children will be challenged by a profusion of races and cultures. Our children may show us the future even before they become adults.

The numbers are there, so let's take advantage of this abundant youth population and structure recruitment efforts specifically targeted at our youth population. It is imperative that our young people be introduced to library and information science at an early age. Just as other professions are introduced through career days, field trips, and classroom visits by representatives of other professions, library and information science should be no exception. Reaching our youth population at an early age and introducing library and information science as a viable career option is one sure way to heighten the visibility of the profession and attain our long-term goal of increasing the number of people of color entering the library profession.

To spread the word about the library profession, we need to target outreach programs to the full range of the population, starting with junior high and high school students. The American Library Association in collaboration with local and state library organizations must initiate a program that encourages our minority students to pursue a college education and consider a career in library and information science. Library professionals of all ethnic backgrounds must visit high schools across the country with large minority enrollments. Many students are still impressed with visitors who represent an organization and are professionally attired.

A Teen Perspective

In 1993, the American Library Association held its annual conference in New Orleans, Louisiana. There were four presenters at a minority recruitment program intended to provide the audience with innovative approaches to recruiting ethnic minorities to the library and information science profession. One presenter, Golda B. Jordan, an African American high school librarian from the state of Louisiana, brought five of her students to the conference. She explained how important it was for the library profession to pique the interests of high school students when addressing the issue of ethnic minority recruitment. She shared with the audience a unique program that she initiated in an attempt to interest more young African American high school students in library and information science. She identified fourteen promising students she felt would be excellent candidates for higher education and who also displayed an interest in libraries and the library profession. The Patterson High Library Media Club was formed, and Jordan and the students met twice weekly. She led discussions, invited outside library professionals to visit the Club, and discussed career opportunities and pertinent issues involving the library profession in general. The Club was also taken on numerous field trips to public, academic, and corporate libraries, where the students had the opportunity to interview the librarian in charge of each institution. She subscribed to professional library publications such as *American Libraries* and *Library Journal* and kept members of the Club abreast of current events involving the library world in general.

At the conclusion of her presentation, she announced that five of the members of the Club were in the audience and she asked them to come to the podium. Jordan had made it possible for these members of the Club to come to the national conference and interact with professionals and nonprofessionals of the library industry. Each student was asked to share his or her experience as a member of the Patterson High Library Media Club and explain why he or she thought library and information science was such a worthwhile and challenging career option. All students expressed their appreciation to Jordan and recognized her as an excellent role model and mentor; they publicly thanked her for her guidance and commitment to the profession and to young people. All students indicated that upon completing undergraduate school, they would be submitting their application for graduate studies in library and information science.

A month after the conference, one of the presenters received this very interesting and encouraging document from two of those students who attended the conference as members of the Patterson High Library Media Club:

RECRUITMENT AND THE FUTURE OF LIBRARIES:
TEENS' PERSPECTIVE

by Evet Mouton and Keia Johnson

We are members of the Patterson High Library Media Club, Patterson, Louisiana, a chapter of the Louisiana Teen-age Librarians' Association. Founded in 1949, the state organization has grown and continues to grow.

It was a fascinating, rewarding, and entertaining experience to have participated in the Young Adult Library Services Association (YALSA) programs during the 112th Annual American Library Association Convention. The convention was held in New Orleans June 24 - July 1, 1993.

We addressed issues and focused on the future of libraries in the year 2000, as well as sharing our ideas and strategies in order to encourage young children and teens to enter the library profession.

On Thursday, June 24, we participated in a pre-conference session and presented views on the topic "Libraries 2000: Planning for Tomorrow's Young Adults Today."

The recruitment assembly was held on Saturday, June 26. The theme was "Recruitment to the Profession: What Can You Do at the State and Local Level?" The recruitment program on Monday, June 28, was smaller and informal. A question and answer session was conducted at the end of the presentation.

Through our experiences and participation in school and public library programs, we are convinced that recruiting young children and teens to the library profession must begin at the pre-kindergarten level and continue through high school and beyond.

We reflect on our early library experiences and participation in school and public library programs in similar and different ways.

"It is real hard to remember my first library experience, but as a young child, I, Evet, do remember having to go to the library for a third-grade assignment. The librarian was friendly and helped by finding several books for my assignment. As I grew older and continued to utilize the libraries, to this day, individuals ask for my assistance. It is really a great feeling!

"I was introduced to books and libraries by my mom at a very young age. We were surrounded by books in the home. Special visits to the public libraries in New Orleans enhanced interest in reading and prepared me to organize my very own library.

"Our weekly visit to the supermarket was a double treat. Not only did I assist my mom with purchasing food for the family, but she allowed me to select a book as a special reward."

"One of the most exciting experiences was the time I, Keia Manika Johnson, received my first library card. I called it a license to read."

As prospective librarians, our concern is the recruiting process as seen through the eyes of teens. Therefore, it is essential to address some important questions as they relate to the ongoing campaign to entice these young people to the field. The questions are:

1. Why is it necessary to recruit young children and teens to the library profession?

2. What is presently being done to generate interest and participation in the field?

3. What are the anticipated plans to insure these youngsters that by the year 2000 libraries will remain a reality?

We were amazed that the American Library Association permitted teens an opportunity to share their views concerning the recruitment and the future of libraries by the year 2000. The delegates were asking questions, taking notes, and making requests during the programs.

We posed two important questions to the group:

1. What can you do as an individual to make sure that libraries continue to play an important role in the educational process?

2. Where do you start?

The recruitment plan must be addressed as a team effort with all library parties and organizations sharing the responsibility for the success of the campaign.

School-Based Level

At the school-based level, the library media specialist must take the initial steps in the recruitment programs for pre-kindergarten through twelfth grades.

Library media specialists, what can you do?

1. Teach library media and especially research skills.

2. Offer college-bound elective courses.

3. Organize library media clubs.

4. Conduct recruitment workshops and media fairs.

5. Host authors and illustrators for special and seasonal programs.

6. Join your state teen library association (if available).

7. Publicize library media activities.

8. Select an outstanding club member of the month.

9. Award a scholarship to an outstanding graduating senior library media club member.

The library media specialist can play a major role in the recruitment process by organizing a club for volunteer library assistants.

During the last few years, the Patterson High School Library Media Club has sponsored recruitment programs, Kindergarten Day, Adopt-a-Child, Adopt-a-Third World Country, and student/faculty in-services.

Each year a Recruitment Day is staged on our campus for parish [county] students. The idea is to stress the role of the library as it relates to the school's success. Several stations are set up in the [recruitment] center. Presenters discuss their particular topics and the participants rotate every few minutes to another station.

The recruitment stations are:

1. Know your library

2. Librarianship as a career

3. Caldecott award winners

4. Newbery award winners

5. Dewey Decimal classification

6. Library of Congress

7. Duties and responsibilities of local and state officers

8. Duties and responsibilities of local and state committee chairs

9. Parliamentary procedure

10. Louisiana Teen-age Librarians' Association

The recruitment program ends with a "mock" convention. The convention is based on the Louisiana Teen-age Librarians' Association. This activity generates interest as well as participation among the students and library media specialists.

At the conclusion of the mock convention, club members and their sponsors are eager to join the state teen organization and go to the convention.

Kindergarten Day, an annual observance of National Library Week, is held in April. Students and teachers are transported to the high school by buses for educational and entertaining activities. The youngsters are entertained by storytellers, authors, artists, Just Say "No" Drug Puppets, and clowns. They participate in skits, question and answer sessions, classroom visitations, and athletic activities. At the end of the program, the visitors are served refreshments. Area businesses and individuals donate gifts for the children and their teachers.

During the 1993 Kindergarten Day program, our club played host to three hundred students and teachers. What a challenge!

The Adopt-a-Child program (ages 6-11) is held during a holiday. Each library media club member and/or library science member is required to adopt a child, sign a contract with the parents, plan library-related activities, provide entertainment, and maintain a scrapbook. All plans are submitted to the librarian for final approval.

This year our club participated in two very special projects. The group collected boxes of books for an Adopt-a-Third World Country activity in conjunction with a program sponsored by Grambling State University, Grambling, Louisiana.

We feel that it is important for the library media specialist to keep the faculty as well as the students abreast of and involved in library activities.

At the beginning of the 1992-93 school year, club members asked the principal for permission to hold in-service workshops for the faculty and students. He agreed. The club selected the theme "Multicultural Extravaganza: Meeting Diverse Needs of Students through Information Power." The culminating program was held February, 1993, from 9 A.M. to 2 P.M. in the library. Invitations were sent to all school and public librarians and to Friends of Libraries in St. Mary Parish.

The Center was set up according to different cultures. Group leaders discussed the history, customs, and traditions as well as the most common myths associated with the culture. Everyone learned about and learned to appreciate a little our uniqueness and our similarities and differences. A group of Native Americans from St. Mary Parish, the Chitimacha Indians, came dressed in historical costumes. They were as excited to visit our school as we were to have them participate in the program. The groups were praised for their outstanding planning and implementation of the four in-services during the year. As an award for their performance, the librarian granted the groups permission to prepare food common to the culture. The luncheon was called "A Taste of Diversity."

Ours is a potpourri of activities; therefore, as teenagers and prospective librarians, we challenge library media specialists to explore, to expand, to create, to innovate, and to stimulate your students' intellect. Students are eager to serve. Ask!

Parish/County Library Associations

The Parish/County Library Associations are obligated and should be held accountable to provide leadership in the recruitment objective in order to bring about immediate and positive feedback. The role of the

Parish/County Library Association is an investment in the future of prospective library candidates. What can you do?

1. Support local school library media clubs.
2. Sponsor a parish/county teen organization.
3. Encourage clubs' participation in state teen organizations (if available).
4. Sponsor parish/county recruitment workshops and media fairs.
5. Recognize clubs (pre-kindergarten through twelfth grades).
6. Award a certificate of recognition for membership.
7. Allow club presidents to address the library association.
8. Disseminate clubs' accomplishments in news media.
9. Award a book scholarship to an outstanding graduating library media member.

American Library Association

The American Library Association was founded in 1876 for libraries, librarians, library trustees, and other people interested in library-related areas. As volunteer teen library media assistants, we appreciate the opportunity to share our view on recruiting the "best and brightest" to the profession. A plan of action, timelines, and resources will determine the success of the recruitment programs as well as the future of libraries.

American Library Association, teens across the country need your assistance concerning our future in the field. What can you do?

1. Sponsor a national teen library association of America.
2. Recognize states sponsoring teen library associations.
3. Publish articles by teens in newsletters and bulletins.
4. Appoint the Young Adult Library Services Association (YALSA) to serve as liaison for the American Library Association and state teen associations.

Louisiana Teen-age Librarians' Association (LTLA)

The Louisiana Teen-age Librarians' Association has contributed to the library profession since 1949. What is the LTLA and what is the role of the teen organization? The LTLA [comprises] library media clubs across the state. It is sponsored by the Louisiana Association of School Librarians, a section of the Louisiana Library Association. The direct link between the Louisiana Association of School Librarians and the Louisiana Teen-age Librarians' Association is the Student Relations Committee. The prime responsibility of this committee is to coordinate the activities of sponsors and students into a unified effort to promote worthwhile library programs.

What is the role of the LTLA and its sponsors to ensure that young children and teens pursue careers in the profession? The state organization employs educational, creative, and fun activities throughout the year.

Let's take a look at what is going on in the state of Louisiana.

The LTLA:

1. Holds an annual convention.

2. Conducts executive board meetings.

3. Hosts local and national authors.

4. Provides tours to academic and special libraries.

5. Publishes newsletters.

6. Participates in local, state, and national conferences/conventions.

7. Contributes to the Louisiana Library Association Scholarship Fund.

8. Constructs and presents the state scrapbook to the Louisiana Archives.

9. Is producing a two-part video outlining the history and activities of the organization.

As members of the Patterson High Library Media Club, we hope that the recruitment process will continue and flourish for the betterment of future generations as a whole.

Evet Mouton, 1993 Reporter
Patterson High Library Media Club
Louisiana Teen-age Librarians' Association
1994 President

Keia Johnson, 1993 President
Patterson High Library Media Club
Louisiana Teen-age Librarians' Association
1993 Second Vice-President

Golda B. Jordan, Librarian/Consultant
Patterson High Library Media Club
Louisiana Teen-age Librarians' Association
2525 Main Street
Patterson, LA 70392

This scenario displays the kind of influence library professionals can have on our young people if professionals are truly committed to the issue of recruiting young people of color to the library profession. We have not followed up to see how many of these club members actually completed their undergraduate work and entered library school. The important issue here is that Ms. Jordan invested the time and energy needed to successfully introduce the library profession to African American youth. This is the type of commitment that must be displayed by library professionals so that young people get a clear understanding of the library profession and what it has to offer.

Introducing library and information science as an exciting and rewarding career opportunity for ethnic minority populations is an essential step in designing a successful marketing strategy for the library and information profession. As library professionals, we must work at polishing our image and promote the profession's significance in today's information and technologically driven society. If we are sincere, we must find effective ways to introduce the profession to our young people. The profession must be presented in such a manner that our youth feel confident that becoming a library and information specialist is the correct career choice, one that will bring them the type of overall satisfaction and job gratification that they are expecting.

Historically, there has been a low number of ethnic minority students interested in the library profession. Traditionally, librarianship has not been an obviously attractive field. Students find it more desirable to become lawyers or earn their MBAs. Ignorance about the library profession is a major stumbling block in attracting minorities. Many students today still view library and information science as it was viewed twenty to thirty years ago. They think librarians sit at their desks and read books and occasionally assist patrons. It's not an easily understood profession. We must constantly disprove stereotypes that don't fairly represent librarians today.

Although the profession offers many great opportunities, the problem is relaying the employment opportunities to the students. Minorities look for role models but usually come up empty. There is a lack of role models in general for the minority community. Librarians are not portrayed in the media. There are minority lawyers, doctors, and teachers on television, but not librarians. Kids don't know what the profession has to offer them.

Outreach

To spread the word about library and information science, professionals need to target outreach programs to the gamut of the minority population, starting with junior high and high school students. We need to initiate pilot programs that encourage students to pursue a college education in preparation for a career in library and information science. Bring in minority library professionals to speak to the students at high schools with large minority enrollments. Students are impressed with members of minorities dressing well and being in leadership positions within a profession.

Working with Educators

Students are not the only people who are misinformed about the library profession. High school counselors often view librarianship as a vocational career and talk about it in terms of bookkeeping. To change their views, we must attend annual meetings of high school counselors and educate them about the library profession.

Recruitment beyond the Schools

We must extend the recruitment process beyond the schools. We cannot afford to wait for minorities to come to us. When career fairs are held at schools, students have to sometimes fit the fair into their schedules and make an effort to come to the fair. Instead, we must go to minorities. We must become involved within the minority community. We need to hold career fairs at churches and community centers. We know that students will be at church or a community center, so why not at least make it convenient for them to walk over to our table?

Student recruitment to library and information science must be approached on two levels. First, long-term recruiting should begin in the high schools; we cannot solely depend on university level recruiting to attain an effective recruitment program.

It is absolutely critical that our minority recruitment strategies target high school populations. A combination of seminars and classroom materials aimed at introducing students to library and information science is a sure way to increase awareness of library and information science as a viable career choice.

Second is the university level, through career fairs, special invitations, and frequent and specifically designed visits by library professionals to promote the profession. These visits should be concentrated at colleges and universities with a large representation of minority students. The goal is to establish proactive relationships with college administrators as well as students.

School Visits

Although career day at junior and senior high schools may appear to be the optimal opportunity for library professionals to introduce library and information services as a viable career choice, we feel that it may sometimes be the least appropriate. Career day bombards the students with too many new faces, too many careers to evaluate, and an enormous amount of information to digest within a short period of time. We highly recommend that library professionals make special arrangements with teachers, the school librarian, or the counselor to schedule a time to visit students other than career day. Simply contact the school counselor and explain that you would like to visit a few classes and request that the counselor assist in scheduling you with the appropriate teachers and classes. Please insist that the class visits be scheduled for the morning; students seem to be more receptive during the morning hours. Three classes of no more than twenty-five students per class (fewer if possible) provides the opportunity for you to present to a usually very receptive audience. It is extremely important that you not only make a good impression upon the students but on the faculty as well. You want both to feel that you have a very worthwhile message to deliver, that being a library and information specialist provides an exciting and challenging career option. It is our responsibility as library professionals to deliver our message with the kind of vim and vigor that will grasp the attention of the students while we also gain the respect of the faculty and administrative staff of the school. It is imperative that we come prepared, armed with the appropriate attitude and proper ammunition to make a great impression upon all those we encounter during the course of the morning. Successfully grasping the full attention of fourteen- and fifteen-year-old students can sometimes be quite a task. We hope that the following will assist in you making a grand presentation:

Things You Will Need

1. *The appropriate attitude.* We must project a very positive attitude in delivering our message to those we are attempting to reach, the students. Students know when you are sincere about your message. If you feel uncomfortable around young people, you should

not be making the presentation. Have someone on your staff who is upbeat and enjoys interacting with kids make the visit. The goal here is to establish a personal relationship with the students while also introducing yourself and the profession.

2. *A quality recruitment video no more than twelve minutes in length.*

3. *Support materials for the video that provide pertinent information about the career.* Hand-outs can be kept by the students. Be sure that your name and telephone number accompany the brochure so that students can make follow-up contact.

4. *Give-aways.* Bring some inexpensive gifts that will appeal to students. Don't just pass them out to each student—have a raffle of some sort. Teenagers love raffles. It's a great attention getter. Don't forget about bookmarks and posters.

5. *Boom box.* You must have music. Usually jazz or popular music sets the stage and stimulates those listening.

6. *A minority library professional (usually the most popular with minority students).*

7. *Twenty to twenty-five students.*

Making Your Presentation

We recommend that you dress in a relaxed manner. A man may wear a tie, and be sure that your overall appearance is neat but relaxed. It is important that the teacher introduce you to his or her students. Try to avoid introductions by the school counselor or principal because students in most cases have a special bond with their teacher. After being introduced, turn your music on at a medium sound level and begin sharing your personal background with the students. Not as a library professional, but information regarding your childhood, where you were born, where you grew up, where you attended junior and senior high school, and where you attended college.

When presenting to minority students, a minority librarian can usually be much more effective. The cultural connection is very important because students can relate and feel comfortable from the very start of your presentation. We need more ethnic minority librarians.

As you continue to share information about yourself, start passing out the raffle tickets. Have one of the students assist you to make sure that each student receives a ticket. As you continue to talk, they will curiously ask, "What are the tickets for? Are we going to win something? What's going on?" Don't respond at this time, but continue to distribute the tickets and share information about yourself. If you played sports or a musical instrument during your junior and senior high school years, share the experience with the students. Ask if any of them play sports or a musical instrument. When the question is asked, almost all students respond that they have either played a sport or an instrument at one time. Pick out one of the students with an affirmative response and ask, "What sport or instrument do or did you play?" This sharing of activities and interests should continue for about five minutes. We have found that many kids love to boast about their personal achievements, especially in the areas of music and sports. Once you have gained their attention, present a second question: "How many of you like music?" I assure you that every hand in the room will be raised. Ask if they like certain types of music and cover each form individually, for example: "How many of you like rock 'n' roll? How many of you like classical music? How many like gospel? How many of you like reggae? By the way, what is reggae music? How many of you like rhythm and blues? How many like country-western?" By this time most of the students have responded to one or more types of music and you have gained their full attention. When you ask, "How many of you like rap?" every hand will be raised and most students will almost be standing in the chairs.

Now is the time to share with them the kind of music you enjoy, the musical form that is playing in the boom box, the music that has been playing in the background while you were presenting. "How many of you like jazz? That's a Miles Davis CD playing. Anyone here know who Miles Davis is? What instrument does he play? Is he still living?"

You really should have the kids on the edge of their seats by now. They will be anxious to find out what the raffle tickets are all about. Inform the students that now is the time for the raffle. Pull out your tickets and have a student assist you in selecting the tickets for your give-aways. The give-aways can be a popular teen magazine, a key chain, tickets to a movie or sports event. The students get a rush from the possibility of possessing the winning ticket. The value of the give-away is secondary. In a class of twenty to twenty-five students, provide about six or seven prizes for the raffle.

When the drawing is completed, you are ready to pose the question: "How many of you have ever considered a career as a librarian, a career in library and information science?" The response is usually overwhelmingly negative, but now you are positioned to share all the great things about the field of library and information science. Introduce your recruitment video and leave time for questions and answers following the video presentation. At the conclusion of the video, distribute support materials that will stimulate the question and answer period. As mentioned earlier, make sure your name and telephone number are listed on the brochure. After the question and answer period, thank the class for their attention and invite them to visit you at the library. In every presentation that we have conducted, at least four or five students out of a class of twenty-five have been interested enough to take the time to visit the library and meet with us personally. Thank the teacher and the administration of the school and request another visit in the very near future.

This is simply one of many ways of introducing the library and information profession to ethnic minority students. You are the one to best judge the most effective approach to students within your community. This approach has worked for us. We sincerely hope that a similar approach to the recruitment of young people will work for you. Good luck!

Community College Students

A gold mine of potential librarians is community college students. Students at community colleges have decided they want to go to college, but have not necessarily decided on a career. It is up to the library profession to tell these students about library and information science. Community colleges can be one of our best markets. Seminars at community colleges, possibly with a panel of library professionals ranging from special librarians to corporate librarians, will enable students to see how librarianship fits into a wide variety of careers.

A Little Excitement, Please

The library profession can be as exciting as we choose to make it. We will not attract the best and the brightest of our ethnic minority population with the same trite and tired messages of the past. No longer is it enough to talk about the rewards of helping a patron find that elusive piece of information or assisting a student in locating the last resource needed for his or her term paper. While these things are certainly important, they are not enough to appeal to our young people. It is imperative that we provide more information about the diversity of skills needed in the library profession—the business and budgeting skills, the human resource skills, as well as the technological skills.

The library industry is a business. Librarians would do well to look at the library profession as part of the business world. Not only would it help to attract students to the profession, it would enable us to apply some of the more successful models of the business world to our efforts of recruiting, mentoring, and ultimately retaining a more diverse population within the profession.

Get Them Early

If we can make students aware of the library profession at an early age, we can make a difference. We need a well-structured program sponsored by the American Library Association that links a number of high schools with the library profession. Local professional library organizations might establish a paid intern program focused on minority students at high schools and at colleges. This would provide high school students with a genuine and overall introduction to the library, not simply traditional employment as a page. Students need to be introduced to and experience working in all phases of librarianship if possible. There is a need to recruit students in their junior and senior high school years who will continue employment through college.

Library Visits

Ethnic minority students need the opportunity to visit various libraries and witness operations and services first hand. We could consider hiring minority interns at the high school level not just as library pages but to train them to work in more challenging positions within the library. We need to expose our young minority students to new opportunities, to help kids feel that there's a place for them within the profession.

A Pre-College Library Program

Possibly a pre-college library program can be developed, focusing on library and information science career enrichment sessions for minority students in the ninth to twelfth grades as high school academic preparation. What courses in high school should a student take if he or she seeks to pursue a career in library and information science? Scholarships and financial assistance help students focus on their academic studies. These help prepare students for matriculation in the university setting.

Bringing local high school students into the library profession might be one answer to easing the minority labor shortage within the profession, but planning is important. Here are some guidelines to ensure that the experience is positive for everyone:

1. *Define roles:* Talk to library staff and clearly state the responsibilities of the students. Make sure everyone feels comfortable with having high school students aboard. If there is a problem, deal with it before the student joins the group.

2. *Keep schedules flexible:* The first priority of students should be schoolwork. During exams or other busy periods, library managers need to be flexible and supportive.

3. *Don't forget the red tape:* Students have a limited amount of hours they can legally work. Make sure the human resources group researches all laws and tax requirements for student employees. Keep the lines of communication open. Managers should keep in close contact with the student and the high school program coordinator during the placement. If expectations are not being met, another placement is unlikely.

4. *Create alternative social gatherings:* To give students the full experience of being part of the library, don't forget to include them in appropriate social functions. If there's an interest in retaining them after high school or during college, show them the fun side of your group.[4]

Student Internships

Professions that have experimented with internships say the students' contagious enthusiasm, ample training, and acquired professional demeanor can add greatly to a team of library professionals. Yet there could be potential problems if the internships are set up incorrectly. Cultural differences that accompany the large age gap, as well as pay scale issues and the fact that these youngsters need mentoring, can put added strain on an already strapped management staff. You must keep in mind that these are high school students, and you must do as much work as possible ahead of time to prepare for them.

Infusing libraries with the fresh enthusiasm of college or high school students can assist the library in becoming a better workplace. Often, it's the perfect catalyst for getting companies to reevaluate the corporate culture and make it more appealing. Libraries must first define their own business culture before we can go out and sell the profession. Younger employees make things more interesting for everyone because they bring a new perspective.

That's the case at Stream International, Inc., a provider of outsourced technical services in Canton, Massachusetts. There, a senior at West Bridgewater High School and six other students play a role in running the help desk—and in boosting company morale. These students bring a real enthusiasm with them to work. They are excited about what they are doing and it shows, explained Tim Minarick, who manages the interns.

The student's intern assignment at Stream calls for him or her to work four days a week, from 3 to 7 P.M., answering incoming help-desk calls. Since each student had to go through the same interview process as any other Stream employee, his or her skills and abilities are on a par with the rest of the staff. He or she is also required to take mandatory training before being allowed to answer calls on a specific product. The student is sometimes paid the going rate for someone in this position.

Cigna, an insurance company in Philadelphia, is working with a group called Inroads, Inc., to recruit students in their junior and senior high school years who will continue employment through college. One of the reasons Cigna managers like working with the Inroads program is that the program prepares the students socially to fit into the group. This is a success because the students are very qualified and interested in working and are prepared to enter the work environment.

Preparation includes mandatory seminars given by the Inroads staff, which teach students how to interview, dress for success, write a résumé, and research a company. The Inroads program is free for students, but companies wishing to sponsor a student pay the student's salary, along with a sliding fee, which is determined by location. Currently, the annual fee in the Philadelphia area is $3,600. Inroads has offices around the country, with its headquarters in St. Louis.

Successful programs such as Stream International and Inroads don't just happen, however. CEOs and executives can foster their growth by offering guidance to local communities and by collaborating with regional schools. Often, all it takes is teaming up with guidance counselors at the local high school or making a trip to address the local parent-teacher organization.

It is just as important to educate the community about the opportunities that are out there as it is to capture the imagination of the students.

Even with the right preparation, there still can be problems when tapping the high school resource pool. Other employees may resent having to work with students. It is always best to meet with the staff and make sure they are comfortable with the situation. In some instances employees have resisted, and there is a need to keep students separate from staff members who are not willing to support the effort.

Library managers also need to be realistic about the time investment necessary for working with students. This is a commitment. Everyone needs to understand that fact. Meet with school representatives and students well in advance of any assignment, clearly stating the goals and interviewing possible applicants thoroughly to ensure the right candidates are chosen.

It is essential that your library have automatic follow-up with school officials to make sure everyone's goals are being met. Also, build some type of accountability into the program to avoid students dropping out of the program.

Remember Culture

The library profession must also contend with culture. Minorities have peer pressure to stay within their neighborhood. Sometimes the connecting link between their neighborhood and preparing for a profession is weak. We need to invade ethnic minority culture. We need to encourage and support individuals' decisions to get an education.

Although colleges in general have a lackluster record of attracting and holding minorities, a number of programs are starting to chip away at the problem. In some areas, college-public school partnerships seek to get minority students thinking about higher education at an early age and to nurture that goal through high school. Once kids have the fever for college, you can do a lot of good.

Many programs court only the academically gifted, but there are exceptions. There have been programs launched aimed at tenth-graders who rank in the top 30 percent of their class but fall short of the top 10 percent. Public school teachers select the students and accompany them to the campus for two weeks of classes and counseling. In order to maintain the students' interest in college, professors and minority alumni correspond with them throughout high school and hold twice-yearly reunions.

Since 1984, Arizona State University has run an innovative program to recruit Hispanic women. Several times a year, Hispanic mothers and their daughters, who range in age from thirteen to eighteen, come to campus to take classes together. Although the purpose is to make parents advocates of college for their girls, 30 percent of the 234 mothers have been sufficiently inspired to continue their own educations. Traditional Hispanic family values encourage females to get married and stay home, and many participants felt that they might not have gone to a four-year college without the program.

Although such efforts hold out hope for improvement, much more needs to be done. By the year 2020, 35 percent of the American population will be minority, with Blacks and Hispanics making up the largest portion. For society's sake as well as for their own survival, colleges cannot afford to have more than a third of the nation view them as inaccessible or inhospitable. Many of the current programs seem to be on the right track, but they will take time to produce results. If higher education is interested in the harvesting of minority students, we have to get in on the planting.[5]

NOTES

1. Joe Schwartz and Thomas Exter, "All Our Children," *American Demographics* 11 (May 1989): 35.
2. Ibid., 34.
3. Ibid.
4. Aileen Crowley, "High School Heroes," *PC Week* 15 (April 13, 1998): 69.
5. Susan Tifft, "The Search for Minorities: Despite Increased Wooing, Few Go On to College," *Time* 134 (Aug. 21, 1989): 64.

5

Library Schools and Recruiting Ethnic Minorities

One Author's Experience: Gregory Reese

I enjoyed going to library school and received my MLS from Case Western Reserve University. I had great professors and enjoyed one professor in particular who made it a point to frequently take his students out of the classroom setting and into the field. During these field excursions, we would visit various libraries, meet with library managers, and discuss library operations. I was the only African American in the class, and during our field trips we had the opportunity to visit many libraries including public libraries located in African American communities.

Unfortunately, the libraries within the African American communities were under siege by the director of the city's large urban library system. The library administration felt a need to close the facilities due to lack of usage. They felt that African Americans did not regard libraries as important and to close the facility would not create a hardship for the African American community. It was simply a poor investment to pay for gas, electricity, and staff of a facility that was not being utilized or appreciated by members of the community. In their opinion, libraries were designed for the educated elite, the well-to-do, the white members of our society. One branch being considered for closing was one I visited as a child, located only a few blocks from where I lived. This was a tragic dilemma, one I felt obligated to address. I had a personal responsibility at stake here, to alter this antiquated and ridiculous trend of thinking that might eventually eliminate the presence of public libraries in our African American communities.

A month or so later, I completed my graduate work and received my MLS. I was honored to have successfully completed graduate school, to receive my MLS and to drop the title of paraprofessional forever. Yet, the closing of these branch facilities never left my mind. After three months of tossing the issue around in my head, I decided that I would investigate applying for admission to the Ph.D. program in library and information science. Enrolling in the program would provide the opportunity to further my education, and in doing so, I would have the opportunity to address the issue involving the library closings from a scholarly perspective.

I scheduled an appointment with the assistant dean and we met in his office shortly after. I shared my desire to enter the Ph.D. program, and the dean was supportive until we discussed my area of concentration following my course work. I explained that I wanted my thesis to concentrate on "The Survival of Public Libraries in African American Communities." His immediate response was, "Why?" I shared my experience while in graduate school and my concern over the possible closings. I explained that knowledge gained through my research while in the Ph.D. program might enable me to assist in keeping the doors of these libraries open. He promised to meet with me within a couple of days and discuss the matter further. At that meeting, he indicated that he had no problem with me entering the Ph.D. program. My graduate grades and other contributions to the university had worked in my favor. But he had a problem with the topic I had selected for my thesis. Our meeting lasted for an hour. I attempted to explain why this issue was important to me and to the African American community as a whole. I remember his closing remarks as if all this took place yesterday: "Mr. Reese, we will gladly accept you into the program but you will have to select another area of study once your course work is completed. We don't view this issue of library closings to be of any real significance, and I think you are concerning yourself with a situation that is out of your control and actually probably going nowhere. Why don't you consider another area of study?" I responded by explaining the importance of this issue and that decisions made presently regarding the closings would surely have a devastating impact on library service in the future within the African American community. He responded, "Well, I can't help you. Besides, we don't have an advisor who could work with you in this area. I'm sorry. If you decide not to change your mind about your thesis, I cannot enroll you into the program. You think about it."

I never entered the Ph.D. program at Case Western Reserve University. Another case in which an opportunity to move an African American through the ranks of our profession was stifled by prejudice and ignorance. Another racist decision made by a racist individual with no inkling of the issue and absolutely no compassion for the opinion or views presented by a minority colleague. Another example of why it is essential that we have more ethnic minority faculty and advisors present in our library schools today. Students at many universities are no longer advised by faculty but in anonymous, often understaffed advising centers. The link with a faculty member is particularly salient in retaining minority students and women. There is a need for minority faculty who understand the problems faced by minority students. Faculty must be sensitive to the needs of minority students and make a special effort to make personal contact with them. Aren't faculty members supposed to be the most memorable part of an educational experience? The number, quality, and interests of the faculty give a school its character. In any profession, it is frequently the full-time faculty who are the major source of the basic research that advances the knowledge base for practice. Since this is not the case, minority students need access to minority professionals in the local area to help eliminate the lack of role models. Having these minority professionals serve as adjunct professors would not be a bad idea.

If a truly diverse faculty is our goal for our nation's library schools, it is time to shift our emphasis from a search and hiring process to the preparation of minority students for academic success. It requires that we take more responsibility for the problems surrounding ethnic minority achievement, not necessarily as a national problem, but campus by campus, department by department, program by program.

I missed the opportunity to obtain my Ph.D., but I did not turn my back on the issue of the library closings. I decided to investigate this matter independently. I needed some answers. I was determined to conjure up as much resistance as possible concerning the issue of the closings. I decided that I would visit and interview the branch managers of the libraries being considered for closing.

Edith Spronz

My first visit was to a community library located in an urban poor African American community managed by Edith Spronz. Spronz, a white middle-aged librarian, had worked throughout the library system for twenty-five years. She had been recently assigned to this particular branch and had been there less than two years. I made an appointment to visit her. I explained that I was a recent graduate of the library school working on a project concerning inner city libraries and I needed her opinion on some library-related issues. She agreed to the appointment and we met one Monday, toured the library, and began our discussion in her office.

My first question was, "How do you like working here at the Clark Branch Library and how long have you been here?" She replied that she loved her job and enjoyed working at the branch with the exception of a few minor concerns. I asked her to elaborate on the few minor concerns and she began to expound on the negatives. "Well, I've tried everything humanly possible to make this place work. It seems that the people in this community don't take advantage of library services. Maybe they just do not like libraries, I just cannot figure it out. This place is basically a hang-out for the kids after school. I can't control the youngsters, and I am actually afraid of many of them. For the most part, no one takes advantage of the book collection. (Note: The book collection is the result of a central-ized selection process, with materials not tailored to meet the specific needs of the community.) Very few young people or adults attend library programs. We have a handful of mothers who occasionally bring their children to story hour. I am just sort of fed up with the whole situation. It took me three weeks to design this travelogue on Switzerland. I even in-cluded some artifacts borrowed from the art museum. We designed press releases, sent out public service announcements, and the staff designed fly-ers that were distributed throughout our library. We even sent three hun-dred flyers to the local high school. Yet the evening of the program, five people were in attendance, and three of the five were members of the staff. I am certain that the members of this community do not realize the im-portance of this institution and what it has to offer. I've given up on trying to increase program attendance, and circulation is a whole other story. I give up! Who are you, anyway?" She reacted as if she had shared too much; her personal resentment engulfed the conversation. She was pretty darn angry by the time I left. This library was one of thirty-three branch facilities within a large urban library system.

Ms. Spronz is an example of a library professional who has absolutely no business serving as manager of this particular branch facility. She has no connection or rapport with the community to which she is attempting to provide service. She is uncomfortable with the people and the community and those who suffer are the African American members of this community.

We Don't Want No Computer

John C. Everette, an African American public library director, was very much in tune with the community in which he worked. It is an ideal situa-tion when an ethnic minority library professional can clearly recognize the shortcomings of the community and can design a plan to emphasize the importance of libraries and its many services. Everette attended elementary, middle, and junior high school within the community, and he savored the opportunity to provide quality library service to this African American urban poor community of 34,000 residents. Introducing computer technology to the residents of this community was a challenging and sensitive issue. The majority of residents within this community were not computer literate and worked up plenty of resistance to the introduction of computer technology. Everette was very much aware and understood the community resistance to technology, yet he felt obligated and challenged to find ways to dismantle the barriers of intimidation that confronted this economically and educationally distressed African American community.

He solicited funds to establish a Technology Center that would offer free introductory computer classes to all who cared to participate. Within this Technology Center would be a computer lab with 30 computers. A full-time instructor was hired, and residents simply called or came to the library to register for the free classes. Residents responded to the opening of the Technology Center in the following manner:

1. Fifteen percent of the community welcomed the Center and were eager to get registered for classes. These were members of the community who had limited knowledge of the importance of computer technology and were anxious to learn more about computers.

2. Sixty percent of the community were not familiar with computer technology but welcomed the opportunity to learn more. They asked questions, got answers, and eventually enrolled in the program.

3. The remaining 25 percent strongly resisted introducing computer technology to their community library. They were highly intimidated by the thought of new technology and felt that John was attempting to convert their traditional library into a video arcade. They were concerned about story hour being eliminated along with the rearrangement of books and materials. John, being African American and very much aware of the cultural and intellectual backgrounds of his constituents, understood that the root of this problem was the fear of the unknown, the fear of computer technology.

This is exactly why it is imperative that we have more ethnic minority library professionals as managers of libraries in ethnic minority communities. Everette announced to the community that he would call a meeting and invite members of the community to come and get a clear understanding of his intentions. More than seventy mostly hostile residents attended the meeting. Yet at the conclusion, Everette convinced the residents that computer technology was the wave of the future and that all members of the African American community needed to be aboard the information super-highway. Moved by his presentation, those in attendance signed up for library cards and registered for the introductory computer classes.

Following is a letter received by Everette just before he decided to hold the meeting. We have inserted the letter just as it was written with the exception of names and addresses. Please note the tone of the letter and how poorly it was written. This clearly demonstrates the need for literacy training, computer technology and other forms of instruction that will support the educational needs of urban poor communities nationwide. It also demonstrates the need for library professionals that can communicate and interact on all levels with members of ethnic minority communities. Mrs. Starks is the branch manager of the facility in which the Technology Center was to be installed, and *The Plain Dealer* and *Call & Post* are local newspapers.

The second letter is one received by Everette from the mayor regarding the importance of libraries within African American communities.

Voters of the Community Library
P.O. Box
Anytown, OH

Dear Mrs. Starks

Wem are tod on our street that the books will be take of the library floor for room for computers. Will this happen in our library. We pay tax here for the books in this library. We pay tax for the furnitur and the rest of what is in that library. If he move any book racks furniture or throw out book holder we will picket that library and take it to the plane dealer and every one else we can. We dont want no computer place, we need a library for our kids to learn. We do not want a play place. The schools have computer in every room, we dont need any more computers. We will send this letter to the school board leader plane dealer call post and any other place we no if he take any book racks out of west branch and put in computer. Tell him to buy him a little house and put his computer in if he thik he need them that bad or put them in his community. Do he live in our community. If he dont he bed not touch any of our furniture books that our tax money bought. we mean business on this street and our kids library.

Nrs, Starks where do he live. Do you no when this eill happen. Make sure you tell that Mr. Everette that well we will not loose any books or any book racks form west branch library and he bed not try it. We dont want no computer

The Technology Center and computer lab have become the most popular service within the library. Adults and children of all ages are flocking in to take advantage of this valuable resource. John was applauded for his leadership on this matter and later received the following letter from the mayor of the community:

Mr. John C. Everette, Director
Anytown Public Library
33362 Library Lane
Anytown, Ohio 44112-3891

Dear Mr. Everette,

Thank you for your concern regarding the importance of public libraries to minority communities. Inner-city libraries can only help our African American children get the best education they can and they can also help our adults have access to as much information as possible.

I will consider visiting the Anytown Public Library for further suggestions sometime in the near future.

Sincerely,

Michael R. Jones
Mayor

The lack of ethnic minority librarians in administrative or management positions within the library profession has had a devastating impact on the quality of library service available to the ethnic minority community. Edith Spronz, a white, frustrated, and anxious-to-retire librarian, is sometimes the typical kind of individual who manages many of our libraries in ethnic minority communities around the country. This is often why there continue to be attempts by white public library administrators of large urban library systems either to totally dismantle traditional services or to close the doors of neighborhood libraries that serve these communities. The case of John C. Everette demonstrates how beneficial it can be to have an ethnic minority library administrator who understands and is very much in tune with the climate of the community. The shortage of ethnic minority staffing in these situations impairs the quality of the library. Lack of minority leadership taints the reality of the situation, giving the false impression that the facility is not being utilized or appreciated by its community. If it were not for the efforts and demands of local ethnic minority educators, politicians, and strong community leaders, the doors of many of these cherished facilities would be closed forever. The closings again are based on the premise that the libraries in ethnic minority communities are not being utilized and to keep these facilities up and operating would not be cost effective.

We are beginning to see an effort being made to recruit minority group members to librarianship and to hire and retain minority librarians. Scholarships, mentoring programs, postgraduate internships, and affirmative action hiring practices are among the techniques that have the potential to assist with increasing the number of minority librarians and promoting a culturally diverse workforce. There is a very real need to funnel more minority students into the pipeline of graduate school programs in library and information science in order to produce more ethnic minority librarians.

Because of imperative societal changes, adequate preparation of minorities for public service in the twenty-first century requires that American colleges and universities structure public service educational programs to train minority administrators capable of managing a multicultural workforce and of serving an ethnically diverse population.

We need African, Asian, Hispanic, and Native American library professionals available to serve their respective communities. Until we get more ethnic minority library managers and staff working within our libraries, a problem of limited library service will exist. Library staff must be capable of relating intellectually and culturally with the community the library is serving. It is almost impossible to effectively operate a public library located in an urban poor minority community without minority staff. Sure, the doors of the library will open and close each day, but the quality of service will be stifled. Minority staff can relate to community needs and develop the kind of services and programs, both educational and entertaining, that will attract the minority community to the library. Too many public library facilities are managed by whites who lack the cultural sensibility needed to effectively and successfully manage a library facility within the minority community. Ethnic minority librarians across the country (few that they are) are successfully operating libraries in our ethnic minority communities. We just don't have enough of them.

It is our responsibility as professional librarians to ensure that more minority librarians are brought into the profession. Library schools play a significant role in the process. Once they are in the profession, we should encourage them to seek management positions. They are desperately needed to replace the likes of the Edith Spronz librarians who continue to hamper the overall effectiveness of public library service in ethnic minority communities.

The Case of Evelyn P. Jones

Evelyn P. Jones, a thirty-one-year-old African American employee of a large public library system, had served as a paraprofessional in children's services for over eleven years. Through the encouragement of her supervisor, Evelyn decided that the time was right to enhance her career opportunities by applying to library school. Evelyn, an excellent employee, completed the application process, which included very favorable letters of recommendation from her immediate supervisor and the library director. The library's board of trustees, informed of her potential, supported the library director's recommendation to provide financial assistance to Jones through the library's tuition reimbursement program. Jones also included a letter of recommendation from the deputy director of her previous employer. Evelyn had worked seven successful years in children's services at another library system before landing her current position.

The library school to which she applied was the only accredited library school within the state. As usual, the enrollment within the School of Library and Information Science was at an all-time high. The program was filled to capacity with additional applicants anxiously awaiting admission. But of the totality of students enrolled in the program, only two were minority, and they were foreign students enrolled through an exchange program. The library program had no American ethnic minority students, and there had been very little effort to recruit them.

College administrators and faculty members must increase the recruitment of U.S. minority group members into graduate programs and limit their admissions of foreign graduate students. The federal government should shift its funding from research grant stipends that finance foreign graduate students to institutional training grants that encourage U.S. minority students to seek graduate education. High-level college administrators should become more directly involved in graduate admissions. Faculty members must actively encourage minority students to pursue graduate studies.

Jones's application was rejected. Her transcript reflected a grade point average (GPA) of 2.4 at the time of her graduation twelve years earlier from an undergraduate program located within the same state as the library school. Admission to the library school was granted to only those applicants who had an undergraduate GPA of 2.8 or higher or who had a graduate degree with a GPA of 2.8 or higher.

Library professionals involved in supporting Jones throughout the application process were concerned that this seemingly excellent candidate for library school was denied admission. With no African American library students enrolled in the program, one would think that Jones's application would have been given special consideration. No consideration was given to the fact that she had over eleven years of work experience as a paraprofessional in two highly respected public library systems and that she had submitted strong letters of recommendation from the deputy director and library director of those libraries. The library school, including its dean, did not feel that there was any immediate need to enroll minority students and flatly refused to reconsider her application. The school felt that the current program was successful in providing quality library professionals needed to serve our educational institutions and public library systems. There was absolutely no need, in the school's view, to make any special effort to recruit minority students, although having a few exchange students would satisfy the minority representation quota if questioned.

As a result, Jones's case was closely reviewed by her immediate supporters and other concerned library professionals within the state. A minority recruitment and retention committee was formed and supported by the State Library Council to address the issues of minority recruitment to the library program. The committee's charge was to establish criteria that would fairly examine current admission practices at the library school. Its mission was to recruit quality minority students to the library program without dismantling the current admission standards established by the library school and the university.

After a year of continuous pressure, Jones was eventually admitted to the school on a conditional basis and successfully completed the program. She currently serves as the assistant director of school libraries within a large public school system in one of our country's most populous urban communities.

The letters between supporters of Jones and the library school are shared below. The first letter, generated by Jones's employer, clearly depicts the frustration encountered in his attempt to persuade library school officials that Jones was an excellent candidate for the library program. The second, also written by the employer, acknowledges the fact that his library board had approved Jones's participation in the library's tuition reimbursement program. The last letter is the dean's response to Jones's application for enrollment. This letter was written only after outside pressure was imposed upon the dean and library school.

FARMINGTON PUBLIC LIBRARY
50 East Town Street
Anytown, Ohio 44112

John P. Hudson, Director

Sarah L. Ward
Dean, School of Library Science
Rockside State University

Dear Dean Ward:

It is extremely unfortunate that the School of Library Science will not provide the opportunity for our employee to be admitted to the graduate program at Rockside State University.

The extremely low percentage of minority students in the program should alarm educators and leaders in the library profession. Blacks comprise approximately 6.1 percent of the total workforce of professionals in both public and academic libraries.

Recruitment efforts alone will not increase the number of minority professionals. Such efforts must be assisted by increased funding and financial aid targeted to potential minority professionals and changes in the curricula that attract people who may not find current program offerings relevant to the needs of minority communities. Also, flexible admissions criteria can provide greater access to minorities and other students who comprise one of the "at risk" categories.

I strongly believe that there is an immediate need for the library profession and its concerned partners in higher education and the private sector to develop a concrete program of recruitment, training, development, and encouragement of minority students.

Our employee is a 1979 graduate of Langston University majoring in journalism. Although her grade point average falls below the required 2.8 for admission, admittance should be granted on a conditional basis for the following reasons:

1. Significant Work Experience
   a. Has worked a total of eleven (11) years as a paraprofessional. Seven years at Townsend Public Library and four years at Farmington Public Library. Excellent performance evaluations at both institutions.

2. Strong letters of recommendation
   a. Tom Watson, Deputy Director—Townsend Public Library
   b. Susan Greene, Supervisor of Branch Libraries—Townsend Public Library
   c. John P. Hudson, Director—Farmington Public Library
3. A strong and healthy commitment to the profession and a desire to become a professional librarian.

I am experiencing difficulty finding professional Black librarians to fill positions within our library system. Our libraries employ graduates of Rockside State University and other library schools throughout the nation. Copies of this letter have been mailed to my colleagues. I wonder if other directors and leaders in the profession are experiencing a similar dilemma?

Sincerely,

John P. Hudson, Director
Farmington Public Library

JPH:jph

cc:

Robert Dunn, Director
Harvard Public Library

Michael G. Hampton, Director
Porter Public Library

Kathleen Toombs, Director
Rocky River Public Library

Dan Watts, Director
Carver Public Library

Barbara K. Stone, Director
Antisdale Public Library

Ruth M. Fortune, Director
Evanston Public Library

Charles C. Goode, Director
Kettering Public Library

Janice C. Miller, Director
State Library

Richard T. Jones, State Librarian

John T. Sparks, Consultant
State Library

Patricia Sally T. Thompson,
   President
American Library Association

Dr. Stewart C. Lefkowitz, President
Rockside State University

FARMINGTON PUBLIC LIBRARY
50 East Town Street
Anytown, Ohio 44112

John P. Hudson, Director

Dean Sarah L. Ward
School of Library Science
Rockside State University

Dear Dean Ward:

I am very pleased to inform you that our Library Board of Trustees has approved participation in the Partnership Program with the School of Library Science.

I have selected Ms. Evelyn P. Jones as our candidate for this exciting opportunity. Ms. Jones has consistently demonstrated a desire to enhance her experience as a librarian. She seriously considered graduate school five years ago, but found that she could not afford tuition. The Partnership Program presents a grand opportunity for Ms. Jones and for Farmington Public Library. Of the five librarians presently working in Children's Services, only *one* is a professional librarian. Completion of the graduate program would not only assist Ms. Jones but would increase the level of professionalism within the department. FPL's agreement to assist with tuition includes that the student must work for the library for two years following completion of the graduate program.

I strongly recommend that Ms. Jones be considered for enrollment. She is a mature and dedicated individual who will succeed academically and professionally.

Please contact me if additional information is needed.

Sincerely,

John P. Hudson, Director
Farmington Public Library

JPH/efd

School of Library Science
ROCKSIDE STATE UNIVERSITY
(216) 872-0098

Evelyn P. Jones
5407 Sunnyslope Dr.
Maple Heights, OH 44137

Dear Evelyn:

This morning I had a meeting with Linda Harvard regarding your efforts to get admitted for graduate study in the School of Library Science. We discussed strategies for you to strengthen your academic record.

The following are suggestions that we recommend you follow:

Take one course this summer on the *undergraduate* level on a subject related to your work as a librarian. A junior or senior level course in children's literature would be one option you could consider.

Take one course this fall on the *undergraduate* level, again on a subject that will help you. A junior or senior level course in writing would be useful. There are a lot of intensive writing assignments in graduate school and getting some writing practice in advance would be very useful. For example, at Rockside State there is a junior level course in Advanced Composition. I am sure you can find a similar course at Johnson State University, if that is more convenient for you.

You also need to prepare for the Graduate Record Exam (GRE), which you should plan to take in October. Johnson State may have a study group to help you prepare. You will have to check this out for yourself.

If you follow these suggestions and do well in the two courses and the GRE, you can be considered for admission for the spring 1992 term. Please note that the School of Library and Information Science does not admit students to begin in the spring. However, it would be possible to take some other courses in the spring if you wished, and start library science courses in the summer of 1992.

Even if you follow all the suggestions listed above, there is no guarantee that you will be admitted to the School. All of these efforts will hopefully strengthen your application, however. If you have any questions about the admission process, please call me or Linda Harvard. We both are sincerely interested in helping you help yourself to strengthen your application for admission to the Graduate College and the School of Library and Information Science.

Sincerely,

Sarah L. Ward, Dean

SLW:bfc

cc: Linda Harvard

The tone of Dean Ward's letter clearly lacks the encouragement and enthusiasm of a library administrator interested in recruiting ethnic minority students to the program. Jones was understandably upset and discouraged after receiving this correspondence.

1. *Take two undergraduate courses at another university.* If the undergraduate courses must be taken, why not allow the applicant to take the courses at the school to which she or he is seeking admission? Student has the opportunity to become familiar with the environment, etc.

2. *The assumption is that Ms. Jones has poor writing skills.* To suggest that another course should be taken in the area of writing is ridiculous.

3. *Find a study group at another university to prepare for the GRE.* Why not provide a vehicle for preparation at the university to which the individual is seeking admission?

4. *If you do well in all the courses and the GRE, there is no guarantee that you will be admitted to the School.* How discouraging! Yet these are the types of barriers that ethnic minorities face continuously. How truly unfortunate.

Here again, the importance of having ethnic minority faculty and administrative staff in our library schools who are sensitive to the needs of minority applicants and students is essential. Successful recruitment efforts will not come about unless issues of this nature are properly addressed.

Library educators, librarians, and library managers must realize that there is a critical need for a national commitment to the recruitment and training of underrepresented racial and ethnic groups into library and information science graduate programs.

The need for collaborative recruitment efforts between library practitioners and library educators is great. Without support from graduate schools in library and information science, recruitment efforts will not have any effect. Graduate programs in library and information science must expand funding and financial aid for innovative recruitment programs.

The Financial Barrier

We have discovered that once potential ethnic minority students have decided that they are interested in pursuing the graduate program in Library and Information Science, the greatest obstacle is financial. The successful recruitment, retention, and graduation of students of color depends on greater sums of money being available. Special funding to support library education for ethnic minority students is essential. Library schools must find funding and set aside money for racial and ethnic minority recruitment. We need to increase the amount of grants and scholarships and discourage loans.

Library schools can develop partnership programs in which the employer and university divide the cost of tuition for the student. Tuition reimbursement programs and library science fellowships are avenues that will assist in providing the dollars to support matriculation of more ethnic minorities. Financial assistance would attract minority students majoring in science and other disciplines that are underrepresented in the library school and within the profession in general. Scholarships can provide funds through programs such as the American Library Association's Spectrum Initiative, in which matching funds from library schools are contributed. We can solicit alumni to make financial contributions to support this effort; a special mailing could be made for this purpose. This could increase the number of work-study programs that can assist with generating the dollars needed to support minority students. The Partnership Program provides an opportunity for a minority employee at a participating library to work on a master's degree in library and information science on a part-time basis while remaining employed. The employer and the school each pay half of the student's tuition. The individual selected must be qualified for admission to a school of library and information science.

The Curriculum

The curriculum and activities of library schools have changed radically, sprouting new fields and producing new professionals. The number of students enrolled and the record number of graduates clearly show that library and information studies education is expanding. As both higher education and the professions themselves respond to changing societal needs, programs are established even as others are phased out. The number of students enrolled and the number graduated both show that library/information science (LIS) is expanding. Enrollment is strong and growing, whether you look at the number of students enrolled or their full-time equivalents. Based on these numbers, we can anticipate a good supply of LIS graduates, many of whom will seek employment in libraries—although a growing number will likely target careers in other aspects of information work.[1]

How many of these LIS graduates will be ethnic minorities? Statistical data at the close of this chapter reveals startling information regarding enrollment and graduation of ethnic minorities from schools of library and information science. Curriculum relevance in library and information science programs designed to include issues of race, ethnicity, gender, and sexual orientation may attract more ethnic minorities. More African American students, for example, means demands for more African American faculty and administrators and for more Black-oriented courses. Curriculum relevance in library and information science programs to minority student interests and to services to minority groups would enhance attractiveness of the programs to ethnic and racial minority persons. One particular arena of relevance is the courses offered on outreach programs and services, such as programs and services to special populations (for example, the poor, racial/ethnic minorities, handicapped, aged, and new learners). Services and programs refer to any activity that provides access to information or meets information needs and/or increases cultural awareness.

We need to increase minority faculty recruitment, increase financial assistance to minority students, and continue to support access to higher education rather than seek quality through exclusionary standards at entrance. We must also recognize that the shortage of minority teachers is related to failures at the elementary levels, and that the needs of the entire school system, especially urban schools, must be addressed.

A counseling support service program must be established to avoid revolving-door admission programs and to eliminate low expectations of minority students. Those minority students who do arrive on campus feel isolated; a resurgence of bigotry has caused many to drop out.

Requirement Barriers

Jones's case is typical. Far too many people of color who demonstrate a strong interest in the library profession and in attending library school are refused the opportunity based on standard admission requirements set by the university. GPA requirements, test scores, and primarily the lack of financial assistance sometimes serve as barriers for ethnic minority students. Some library schools across the country are making strides in addressing these roadblocks. Other institutions have decided they will not use the tests, not because they are invalid per se, but because they pose a barrier to the increased admission of minority students. Do qualifications at the time of admission matter? Isn't the important thing what the institutions manage to do with those they admit? If they graduate, are they not qualified? Yes, but many do not graduate. Two to three times as many African American students as white students drop out before graduation. These statistics can be linked to the lack of ongoing financial support and appropriate counseling systems (mentoring) specifically designed for ethnic minority students who have been admitted to the program.

When ethnic minority applicants fail to meet the standard admission requirement(s) set by the university or library school, there should be alternatives. Waive the grade point average (GPA) or Graduate Record Exam (GRE) requirements in special cases in which personal characteristics can be applied. Leadership qualities, social concern as exhibited by community activities, the capacity to overcome adversity, and other non-quantifiable virtues and achievements should be considered. Also, letters of recommendation and on-the-job experience are other factors that can serve as justification for enrolling the student on a *conditional basis only*. Admissions officers should seriously consider these alternatives or merits. Neither undergraduate nor professional school admissions ought to be determined exclusively by test scores or grade-point averages. Although intellectual qualities should be of the first importance, applicants do sometimes display non-intellectual credits that are so unusual as to justify what would otherwise be anomalous action.

At some universities test scores play a role in admissions but only that. They rarely guarantee entry. Test scores become a focus of discussion only when there is a marked discrepancy between an applicant's academic record and test scores. Some admissions committees would rather see a strong transcript and mediocre test scores. Committees should also consider those students who have been movers and shakers—students who have exhibited leadership and may have challenged the status quo. Through the interview process, the committee should look for evidence of a minority student's genuine commitment to the academic field or library profession.

Admission policies are necessary and must be designed to ensure that students of all backgrounds have access to education. A diverse class of students is absolutely essential. If race is eliminated as a consideration, African Americans and other minorities would probably be even more underrepresented on campus. Everyone seeking admission to the library school should be considered on an individual basis, looking at a broad array of factors the university has determined to be relevant: undergraduate grades, test scores, work experience, and letters of recommendation. The focus should be on the individual, not on the minority group as a whole.

When all factors are weighed, if the applicant does not meet any of the established criteria, he or she should not be admitted.

Weighing Diversity

A rarely discussed problem facing university admissions procedures is how much weight to give to diversity. Officials will admit that special consideration is shown to certain ethnic minority groups, and that membership in such a minority group can be an important factor in whether a candidate is chosen over others who may have better academic credentials.

One of the key reasons why we have to evaluate the importance of racial preferences for African Americans is that this country has a special obligation to African Americans that has not been fully discharged. Another is that, at present, a strict application of the principle of qualification would send an inappropriate message to the African American community, a message that may possibly convey lack of sensitivity to their difficulties and problems.

These points of view are rooted in history. African Americans—and the struggle for their full and fair inclusion in U.S. society—have been a part of American history from the beginning. Our Constitution took special—but grossly unfair—account of their status, our greatest war was fought over their status, and our most important constitutional amendments were adopted because of the need to right past wrongs done to them. And, amid the civil rights revolution of the 1960s, affirmative action was instituted to compensate for the damage done to African American achievement and life chances by almost 400 years of slavery, followed by state-sanctioned discrimination and massive prejudice.[2]

Yet today a vast gulf of difference persists between the educational and occupational status of Blacks and whites, a gulf that encompasses statistical measures of wealth, residential segregation, and social relationships with other Americans. Thirty years ago, with the passage of the great civil rights laws, one could have reasonably expected that all would be set right by now. But today, even after taking into account substantial progress and change, it is clear how deeply rooted and substantial the differences between African Americans and other Americans remain.

Nearly all American universities currently seek to achieve an ethnically diverse student body in order to prepare young people to live in an increasingly multiracial and multicultural society. Diversity is usually pursued through "proportional representation," a policy that attempts to shape each university class to approximate the proportion of African Americans, Hispanics, whites, Asian Americans, and other groups in the general population. At colleges and universities where such racial balancing is official policy, an admissions report argues that proportional representation is the only just allocation of privileges for a state school in a democratic society, and moreover, a broad diversity of backgrounds, values, and viewpoints is an integral part of a stimulating intellectual and cultural environment in which students educate one another.

The lofty goals of proportional representation are frustrated, however, by the fact that different racial groups perform very differently on academic indicators used by admissions officials, such as grades and standardized test scores. For example, on a scale of 400 to 1600, white and Asian American students on average score nearly 200 points higher than African American students on the Scholastic Aptitude Test (SAT). Consequently, the only way for colleges to achieve ethnic proportionalism is to downplay or abandon such merit criteria and to accept students from typically underrepresented groups, such as African Americans, Hispanics, and Native Americans, rather than better-qualified students from among whites and Asian Americans.[3]

How, then, should we respond to this undeniable reality? Let standards prevail and enhance the effort to recruit, finance, and retain ethnic minority graduate students. If needed, annually admit a percentage of minority students based on a conditional or provisional basis. The criteria for conditional admittance should be strict and failure to meet academic achievement standards should immediately result in the student's being removed from the program. Those who gain entry will know that they are properly qualified for entry, that they have been selected without discrimination, and their classmates will know too. The result will actually be improved race relations and a continuance of the improvements we have seen in minority performance in recent decades. Fifteen years from now, perhaps 3 or 4 percent of students in the top schools will be minority. And, meanwhile, let us improve elementary and high school education—as we have been trying to do for the last fifteen years or more. It is essential that we improve the quality of education within our minority communities so that our children are adequately prepared for secondary education. This is a responsibility that the federal government along with local legislators and educational leaders within the ethnic minority community must address.

There is a good faith motive to stand up and support diversity within our colleges and universities. What kind of institutions of higher education would we have if African Americans suddenly dropped from 6 or 7 percent of enrollment to 1 or 2 percent? The presence of African Americans in classes immediately introduces another tone, another range of questions (often to the discomfort of African American students who do not want this representational burden placed upon them). The tone may be one of embarrassment and hesitation and self-censorship among whites (students and faculty). But must we not all learn how to face these questions together with our fellow citizens? We should not be able to escape from this embarrassment by the reduction of African American students to minuscule numbers.[4]

Higher education's governing principle is qualification—merit. Should it make room for another and quite different principle, equal participation? The latter should never become dominant. Racial proportional representation would be a disaster. But basically the answer is yes—the principle of equal participation can and should be given some role. This decision has costs. But the alternative is too grim to contemplate.

College campuses are in danger of returning to the kind of overwhelmingly white student bodies they had before the civil rights movement. We need to see diversity achieved through better outreach programs and other approaches that don't necessarily rely on different standards for whites and minorities.

Target-Marketing

As reiterated throughout this work, clearly marketing the library and information science profession to ethnic minority populations will automatically increase the number of applicants to library schools. Many members of ethnic minority groups simply are not aware of the career opportunities available in library and information science. And there has never been a significant initiative to introduce our profession to ethnic minorities. Targeted-marketing is a sure way at least to enhance the number or increase the pool of ethnic minorities who consider a career in library and information science.

Institutions of higher learning have become, for better or worse, the gateways to prominence, privilege, wealth, and power in American society. Our nation must renew its commitment to minorities to achieve full, equitable participation in American life for all American citizens. The schools of library and information science must reaffirm their commitment to increasing minority access to the library and information science profession by adopting a comprehensive program for the recruitment of minorities.

Statistics

Thanks to the 1997 Association for Library and Information Science Education (ALISE) Statistical Report, we are able to provide some valuable statistical information regarding schools of library and information science and ethnic minority participation across the country. Tables 5-1, 5-2, 5-3, and 5-4, described below, are located at the end of this chapter. Data from the "Students" and "Faculty" sections for ALA-accredited U.S. colleges are examined. We hope that the numbers provided indicate the needs, and that they will assist library professionals in addressing the recruitment of minority students and faculty within the schools of library and information science across the United States and Canada.

In reporting ethnic origin the following five categories, as defined by the U.S. Department of Labor, were used:

AI American Indian or Alaskan Native—a person having origin in any of the original peoples of North America who maintains cultural identification through tribal affiliation or community recognition.

AP Asian or Pacific Islander—a person having origin in any of the original peoples of the Far East, Southeast Asia, the Indian subcontinent, or the Pacific Islands. This area includes, for example, China, Japan, Korea, the Philippine Islands, Samoa, and Taiwan. The Indian subcontinent includes the countries of India, Pakistan, Bangladesh, Sri Lanka, Nepal, Sikkim, and Bhutan.

B Black, not of Hispanic origin—a person having origin in any of the Black racial groups of Africa.

H Hispanic—a person of Cuban, Central or South American, Mexican, Puerto Rican, or other Spanish culture or origin, regardless of race. Only those persons from Central and South American countries who are of Spanish origin, descent, or culture were to be included in this category. Persons from Brazil, Guyana, Surinam, or Trinidad, for example, were to be classified according to their race and not necessarily included in the Hispanic category. Additionally, this category did not include persons from Portugal. These individuals would be classified according to race.

W White, not of Hispanic origin—a person having origin in any of the original peoples of Europe, North America, or the Middle East.

I   International students—all students who were not U.S. (or Canadian for Canadian schools) citizens, permanent residents, or landed immigrants.

NA   Students for whom ethnic information was not available.

Students

Table 5-1 provides statistics that represent ethnic minority students who were awarded degrees at each program level, distributed by gender and ethnic origin. A total of 5,881 bachelor's, master's, post-master's, and doctoral degrees were awarded by ALA-accredited schools during 1995-96. Female graduates accounted for 74.3 percent of all degrees awarded. This male-female distribution varies considerably among the different degree programs. From a high of 76.9 percent of ALA-accredited master's degrees and 72.7 percent of doctoral degrees awarded to females, the percentage drops to 54.3, 47.6, and 42 percent for the "other master's," post-master's, and bachelor's degrees respectively.

The figures in table 5-1 also show that the graduates of programs offered by ALA-accredited schools continue to be predominantly white (76.3 percent). Blacks are the largest non-white ethnic group (3.4 percent), followed closely by Asian or Pacific Islanders (3.2 percent). While Blacks were 7.9 percent of the recipients of post-master's degrees, they received only 1.5 percent of the doctoral degrees granted in 1995-96.

Table 5-2 provides statistics that show ethnic minority students enrolled in an ALA-accredited master's program and working toward a master's degree in librarianship, on or off campus during academic year 1995-96. At the ALA-accredited master's degree level, four schools, Dominican University (213), Texas (212), Simmons (206), and Indiana (202) awarded more than 200 degrees. A total of nine of the 56 schools awarded more than 150 degrees. Five schools conferred fewer than 40 degrees (Alberta, Clark Atlanta, Dalhousie, Puerto Rico, and Tennessee).

Table 5-3 shows the ethnic distribution of students pursuing the ALA-accredited master's degree for each school. For the 51 schools that report ethnic data, the 9,888 white students constitute 78.2 percent of the students in those programs. Black students make up 4.1 percent of that enrollment, roughly a third of the 12.7 percent of the 1997 U.S. population estimated by the U.S. Census Bureau to be Black. Hispanic and Asian or Pacific Islanders each comprise 2.7 percent of ALA-accredited master's enrollment, compared with their 10.8 and 3.7 percent respectively of the estimated 1997 U.S. population. Based on the comparison of their percentage of the population with enrollment in ALA-accredited master's programs, students of Hispanic origin are the most underrepresented, followed by Blacks.

When the ethnic composition of each school is examined, some interesting distributions are evident. Schools with a higher number of Black students (more than 25) are limited to programs located in historically Black universities (Clark Atlanta and North Carolina Central) and in some of the universities situated in large metropolitan areas (Catholic, Pratt, Queens, and Wayne State). Only South Carolina, with 24 Black students, has a similar enrollment without having those characteristics. The school with the highest Black ALA-accredited master's enrollment is Clark Atlanta (53). Eleven of the 51 ALA-accredited schools (21.6 percent) reporting ethnic data indicated their Black student enrollment was either zero or one. Figures for the 336 Hispanic students pursuing the ALA-accredited master's degree are heavily skewed, in that 37.2 percent (125) of those students are enrolled at Puerto Rico. Following Puerto Rico, Texas (38) and San Jose (23) have the largest Hispanic enrollments. Three other schools (Pratt, Queens, and South Florida) have more than 15 Hispanic students each. No other school reports more than nine Hispanic students. There are eleven schools with no Hispanic enrollment and another eleven schools with only one Hispanic student each. Taken together, these 22 schools account for 43.1 percent of the schools reporting ethnic data.[5]

Faculty

Table 5-4 shows the ethnic background of full-time faculty in ALA-accredited schools in the United States on January 1, 1997. The schools of the United States were asked to provide ethnic data for their full-time faculty. Forty-eight schools responded to the survey and provided the information in table 5-4. Information on the deans and directors is from 48 schools.[6]

Over the last decade, we have seen the reemergence of barriers that threaten the progress made in equalizing opportunity. Disagreement about the adequacy of federal support for student assistance is the most obvious difficulty. Rising tuition, growing student debt burdens, declining minority participation, increased dropout rates—these are all signs of a decline in access to higher education. These ominous trends come at a time when the job requirements of a technological society are demanding much higher levels of preparation. Between now and the year 2000, according to a recent study sponsored by the Department of Labor, a majority of all new jobs will, for the first time in history, call for some form of post-secondary education.

The need for well-prepared librarians who have compassion for minorities and with whom their patrons can identify is vital. If the current devastating trend limiting educational opportunities for minorities in the library profession continues, minority children will be deprived of their role models and special kind of caring that only librarians from their own racial and ethnic background can provide.

University presidents and chancellors must make a commitment to the recruitment and retention of minority professors. It is critical to increase the presence of minority faculty members and to ensure that the curriculum is attractive to and effective with minorities.

The key factor in the success rate of recruiting racial and ethnic minorities into library and information science programs is the degree to which financial aid is available, including job opportunities for graduate library school students.

Internships and pre-professional work-study opportunities offer excellent opportunities for minority students to earn an income and gain valued experience. Public library systems around the country have had successful librarian trainee programs for many years that offer the opportunity to work in ethnic communities doing professional work while completing library and information science courses. Some libraries pay part-time tuition reimbursement for minority employees. Academic libraries on campuses that have library school programs usually offer tuition reimbursement for full-time employees.

Within the next two decades, one in three United States residents will be a member of a racial or ethnic minority. One of the keys to serve these populations' information needs effectively is to increase the participation of ethnic minorities in library and information services.

Table 5-1. Ethnic Minority Students Awarded Degrees

Degree	Gender	AI	AP	B	H	W	I	NA	Total
ALA-Accredited Master's	Male	6	31	32	30	936	38	143	1,216
	Female	13	110	145	87	3,214	102	384	4,055
	Subtotal	*19*	*141*	*177*	*117*	*4,150*	*140*	*527*	*5,271*
Other Master's	Male	0	9	2	5	82	15	24	137
	Female	1	19	7	0	82	26	28	163
	Subtotal	*1*	*28*	*9*	*5*	*164*	*41*	*52*	*300*
Post-Master's	Male	0	0	3	1	24	4	1	33
	Female	1	0	2	0	17	10	0	30
	Subtotal	*1*	*0*	*5*	*1*	*41*	*14*	*1*	*63*
Doctoral	Male	0	3	0	1	8	3	3	18
	Female	0	9	1	0	31	4	3	48
	Subtotal	*0*	*12*	*1*	*1*	*39*	*7*	*6*	*66*
Bachelor's	Male	0	3	3	0	52	0	47	105
	Female	0	3	2	0	40	2	29	76
	Subtotal	*0*	*6*	*5*	*0*	*92*	*2*	*76*	*181*
Total	Male	6	46	40	37	1,102	60	218	1,509
	Female	15	141	157	87	3,384	144	444	4,372
	Total	*21*	*187*	*197*	*124*	*4,486*	*204*	*662*	*5,881*

AI American Indian or Alaskan Native
AP Asian or Pacific Islander
B   Black, not of Hispanic origin
H   Hispanic
W   White, not of Hispanic origin
I   International student
NA No ethnic information available

Table 5-2. Ethnic Minority Students Working toward an MLS

School	Gender	AI	AP	B	H	W	I	NA	Total
Alabama	Male	0	0	0	0	12	0	0	12
	Female	0	0	4	0	48	2	0	54
	Subtotal	*0*	*0*	*4*	*0*	*60*	*2*	*0*	*66*
Albany	Male	0	2	0	1	15	1	4	23
	Female	0	1	1	0	70	1	21	94
	Subtotal	*0*	*3*	*1*	*1*	*85*	*2*	*25*	*117*
Alberta	Male	—	—	—	—	—	—	9	9
	Female	—	—	—	—	—	—	26	26
	Subtotal	*—*	*—*	*—*	*—*	*—*	*—*	*35*	*35*
Arizona	Male	0	0	0	1	28	4	0	33
	Female	1	2	1	10	102	3	0	119
	Subtotal	*1*	*2*	*1*	*11*	*130*	*7*	*0*	*152*
British Columbia	Male	—	—	—	—	—	—	9	9
	Female	—	—	—	—	—	—	48	48
	Subtotal	*—*	*—*	*—*	*—*	*—*	*—*	*57*	*57*
Buffalo	Male	0	3	2	1	24	0	0	30
	Female	0	2	3	2	84	1	0	92
	Subtotal	*0*	*5*	*5*	*3*	*108*	*1*	*0*	*122*

AI   American Indian or Alaskan Native   H   Hispanic   I   International student

AP   Asian or Pacific Islander   W   White, not of Hispanic origin   NA   No ethnic information available

B   Black, not of Hispanic origin

(Continued)

Table 5-2. Ethnic Minority Students Working toward an MLS *(Continued)*

School	Gender	AI	AP	B	H	W	I	NA	Total
Calif. Los Angeles	Male	0	2	0	3	4	0	0	9
	Female	0	5	2	2	21	1	0	31
	Subtotal	*0*	*7*	*2*	*5*	*25*	*1*	*0*	*40*
Catholic	Male	0	0	1	0	24	2	0	27
	Female	0	4	4	2	61	3	0	74
	Subtotal	*0*	*4*	*5*	*2*	*85*	*5*	*0*	*101*
Clarion	Male	0	0	2	0	15	2	0	19
	Female	0	0	1	0	25	2	0	28
	Subtotal	*0*	*0*	*3*	*0*	*40*	*4*	*0*	*47*
Clark Atlanta	Male	0	1	1	0	1	0	0	3
	Female	0	3	17	0	10	0	0	30
	Subtotal	*0*	*4*	*18*	*0*	*11*	*0*	*0*	*33*
Dalhousie	Male	0	0	0	0	9	0	0	9
	Female	0	1	0	0	27	0	0	28
	Subtotal	*0*	*1*	*0*	*0*	*36*	*0*	*0*	*37*
Drexel	Male	0	1	0	1	18	0	1	21
	Female	0	2	3	0	50	1	6	62
	Subtotal	*0*	*3*	*3*	*1*	*68*	*1*	*7*	*83*

School	Gender	AI	AP	B	H	W	I	NA	Total
Emporia	Male	0	0	0	0	15	2	0	17
	Female	0	1	0	1	85	6	0	93
	Subtotal	*0*	*1*	*0*	*1*	*100*	*8*	*0*	*110*
Florida State	Male	0	1	0	0	29	0	0	30
	Female	0	1	6	3	79	0	0	89
	Subtotal	*0*	*2*	*6*	*3*	*108*	*0*	*0*	*119*
Hawaii	Male	0	4	0	0	5	1	0	10
	Female	0	18	0	0	22	1	0	41
	Subtotal	*0*	*22*	*0*	*0*	*27*	*2*	*0*	*51*
Illinois	Male	0	2	2	0	26	2	0	32
	Female	0	1	3	1	54	13	0	72
	Subtotal	*0*	*3*	*5*	*1*	*80*	*15*	*0*	*104*
Indiana	Male	0	2	0	0	42	2	3	49
	Female	1	2	4	1	133	6	6	153
	Subtotal	*1*	*4*	*4*	*1*	*175*	*8*	*9*	*202*
Iowa	Male	0	0	0	0	8	0	0	8
	Female	0	0	0	1	32	1	0	34
	Subtotal	*0*	*0*	*0*	*1*	*40*	*1*	*0*	*42*

AI   American Indian or Alaskan Native
AP   Asian or Pacific Islander
B   Black, not of Hispanic origin
H   Hispanic
W   White, not of Hispanic origin
I   International student
NA   No ethnic information available

(Continued)

Table 5-2. Ethnic Minority Students Working toward an MLS *(Continued)*

School	Gender	AI	AP	B	H	W	I	NA	Total
Kent State	Male	0	0	1	0	39	2	0	42
	Female	0	1	3	2	132	0	0	138
	Subtotal	*0*	*1*	*4*	*2*	*171*	*2*	*0*	*180*
Kentucky	Male	0	0	0	0	18	0	0	18
	Female	0	0	0	0	71	0	0	71
	Subtotal	*0*	*0*	*0*	*0*	*89*	*0*	*0*	*89*
Long Island	Male	0	0	1	0	12	0	0	13
	Female	0	1	4	1	78	1	0	85
	Subtotal	*0*	*1*	*5*	*1*	*90*	*1*	*0*	*98*
Louisiana State	Male	0	1	0	0	9	2	0	12
	Female	0	0	10	1	46	5	0	62
	Subtotal	*0*	*1*	*10*	*1*	*55*	*7*	*0*	*74*
Maryland	Male	0	0	0	0	20	0	0	20
	Female	0	2	4	0	69	3	0	78
	Subtotal	*0*	*2*	*4*	*0*	*89*	*3*	*0*	*98*
McGill	Male	—	—	—	—	—	—	14	14
	Female	—	—	—	—	—	—	38	38
	Subtotal	*—*	*—*	*—*	*—*	*—*	*—*	*52*	*52*

School	Gender	AI	AP	B	H	W	I	NA	Total
Michigan	Male	0	0	1	2	19	0	5	27
	Female	0	4	2	1	69	0	4	80
	Subtotal	*0*	*4*	*3*	*3*	*88*	*0*	*9*	*107*
Missouri	Male	0	0	0	0	25	0	0	25
	Female	0	1	2	0	66	1	0	70
	Subtotal	*0*	*1*	*2*	*0*	*91*	*1*	*0*	*95*
Montréal	Male	0	0	0	0	19	0	0	19
	Female	0	0	0	0	34	1	0	35
	Subtotal	*0*	*0*	*0*	*0*	*53*	*1*	*0*	*54*
NC Central	Male	0	0	0	0	6	1	0	7
	Female	2	0	11	0	27	3	0	43
	Subtotal	*2*	*0*	*11*	*0*	*33*	*4*	*0*	*50*
NC Chapel Hill	Male	0	0	0	0	14	1	0	15
	Female	0	1	2	0	41	2	0	46
	Subtotal	*0*	*1*	*2*	*0*	*55*	*3*	*0*	*61*
NC Greensboro	Male	0	0	0	0	16	0	0	16
	Female	0	0	2	0	43	0	0	45
	Subtotal	*0*	*0*	*2*	*0*	*59*	*0*	*0*	*61*

AI American Indian or Alaskan Native
AP Asian or Pacific Islander
B   Black, not of Hispanic origin
H   Hispanic
W   White, not of Hispanic origin
I   International student
NA No ethnic information available
(Continued)

Table 5-2. Ethnic Minority Students Working toward an MLS *(Continued)*

School	Gender	AI	AP	B	H	W	I	NA	Total
North Texas	Male	0	1	2	0	28	0	0	31
	Female	1	2	2	2	72	0	0	79
	Subtotal	*1*	*3*	*4*	*2*	*100*	*0*	*0*	*110*
Oklahoma	Male	0	0	0	0	9	1	0	10
	Female	1	0	2	0	42	1	1	47
	Subtotal	*1*	*0*	*2*	*0*	*51*	*2*	*1*	*57*
Pittsburgh	Male	0	1	1	1	20	0	0	23
	Female	0	3	2	0	87	0	0	92
	Subtotal	*0*	*4*	*3*	*1*	*107*	*0*	*0*	*115*
Pratt	Male	0	0	4	2	25	1	0	32
	Female	0	5	7	3	43	1	0	59
	Subtotal	*0*	*5*	*11*	*5*	*68*	*2*	*0*	*91*
Puerto Rico	Male	0	0	0	3	0	0	0	3
	Female	0	0	0	20	0	0	0	20
	Subtotal	*0*	*0*	*0*	*23*	*0*	*0*	*0*	*23*
Queens	Male	0	1	2	1	19	0	0	23
	Female	0	4	7	1	41	0	0	53
	Subtotal	*0*	*5*	*9*	*2*	*60*	*0*	*0*	*76*

School	Gender	AI	AP	B	H	W	I	NA	Total
Rhode Island	Male	1	0	0	0	4	0	0	5
	Female	0	1	0	0	41	0	0	42
	Subtotal	*1*	*1*	*0*	*0*	*45*	*0*	*0*	*47*
Rosary (now Dominican)	Male	0	0	3	0	40	1	0	44
	Female	0	5	0	3	158	3	0	169
	Subtotal	*0*	*5*	*3*	*3*	*198*	*4*	*0*	*213*
Rutgers	Male	0	1	3	1	29	1	0	35
	Female	0	5	4	2	117	3	0	131
	Subtotal	*0*	*6*	*7*	*3*	*146*	*4*	*0*	*166*
St. John's	Male	0	1	0	0	6	1	0	8
	Female	0	1	2	2	32	5	0	42
	Subtotal	*0*	*2*	*2*	*2*	*38*	*6*	*0*	*50*
San Jose	Male	2	4	0	2	28	0	42	78
	Female	2	7	2	3	57	1	23	95
	Subtotal	*4*	*11*	*2*	*5*	*85*	*1*	*65*	*173*
Simmons	Male	1	0	0	0	40	2	0	43
	Female	0	1	3	1	152	6	0	163
	Subtotal	*1*	*1*	*3*	*1*	*192*	*8*	*0*	*206*

AI American Indian or Alaskan Native   H   Hispanic   I   International student
AP Asian or Pacific Islander   W   White, not of Hispanic origin   NA   No ethnic information available
B Black, not of Hispanic origin

(Continued)

Table 5-2. Ethnic Minority Students Working toward an MLS *(Continued)*

School	Gender	AI	AP	B	H	W	I	NA	Total
South Carolina	Male	1	0	3	0	30	2	0	36
	Female	0	2	1	0	99	2	0	104
	Subtotal	*1*	*2*	*4*	*0*	*129*	*4*	*0*	*140*
South Florida	Male	0	0	0	3	27	0	0	30
	Female	0	2	4	1	99	2	0	108
	Subtotal	*0*	*2*	*4*	*4*	*126*	*2*	*0*	*138*
Southern Connecticut	Male	—	—	—	—	—	—	11	11
	Female	—	—	—	—	—	—	60	60
	Subtotal	*—*	*—*	*—*	*—*	*—*	*—*	*71*	*71*
Southern Mississippi	Male	0	1	0	0	9	0	0	10
	Female	0	2	0	0	30	0	0	32
	Subtotal	*0*	*3*	*0*	*0*	*39*	*0*	*0*	*42*
Syracuse	Male	0	0	0	0	15	0	0	15
	Female	0	0	0	0	48	3	0	51
	Subtotal	*0*	*0*	*0*	*0*	*63*	*3*	*0*	*66*
Tennessee	Male	0	0	0	0	7	0	1	8
	Female	0	0	0	0	23	1	2	26
	Subtotal	*0*	*0*	*0*	*0*	*30*	*1*	*3*	*34*

School	Gender	AI	AP	B	H	W	I	NA	Total
Texas	Male	1	1	1	4	42	2	0	51
	Female	3	4	2	17	135	0	0	161
	Subtotal	*4*	*5*	*3*	*21*	*177*	*2*	*0*	*212*
Texas Woman's	Male	0	0	0	0	6	0	0	6
	Female	1	1	1	3	52	0	0	58
	Subtotal	*1*	*1*	*1*	*3*	*58*	*0*	*0*	*64*
Toronto	Male	—	—	—	—	—	—	12	12
	Female	—	—	—	—	—	—	63	63
	Subtotal	*—*	*—*	*—*	*—*	*—*	*—*	*75*	*75*
Washington	Male	0	1	0	2	19	0	0	22
	Female	0	4	1	0	63	0	0	68
	Subtotal	*0*	*5*	*1*	*2*	*82*	*0*	*0*	*90*
Wayne State	Male	0	0	2	0	30	0	0	32
	Female	0	5	13	1	120	0	0	139
	Subtotal	*0*	*5*	*15*	*1*	*150*	*0*	*0*	*171*
Western Ontario	Male	—	—	—	—	—	—	32	32
	Female	—	—	—	—	—	—	86	86
	Subtotal	*—*	*—*	*—*	*—*	*—*	*—*	*118*	*118*

AI American Indian or Alaskan Native
AP Asian or Pacific Islander
B Black, not of Hispanic origin
H Hispanic
W White, not of Hispanic origin
I International student
NA No ethnic information available

(Continued)

Table 5-2. Ethnic Minority Students Working toward an MLS *(Continued)*

School	Gender	AI	AP	B	H	W	I	NA	Total
Wisc. Madison	Male	0	0	0	1	13	1	0	15
	Female	1	3	1	0	43	7	0	55
	Subtotal	*1*	*3*	*1*	*1*	*56*	*8*	*0*	*70*
Wisc. Milwaukee	Male	0	0	0	1	18	4	0	23
	Female	0	0	2	0	81	10	0	93
	Subtotal	*0*	*0*	*2*	*1*	*99*	*14*	*0*	*116*
Total (56 schools)	Male	6	31	32	30	936	38	143	1,216
	Female	13	110	145	87	3,214	102	384	4,055
	Total	*19*	*141*	*177*	*117*	*4,150*	*140*	*527*	*5,271*
Mean (n = 50)	Male	0.12	0.62	0.64	0.60	18.72	0.76		21.71
	Female	0.26	2.20	2.90	1.74	64.28	2.04		72.41
	Total	*0.38*	*2.82*	*3.54*	*2.34*	*83.00*	*2.80*		*94.12* *(n = 56)*

AI   American Indian or Alaskan Native
AP   Asian or Pacific Islander
B   Black, not of Hispanic origin

H   Hispanic
W   White, not of Hispanic origin

I   International student
NA   No ethnic information available

Table 5-3. Ethnic Distribution of Students in MLS Programs

School	Gender	AI	AP	B	H	W	I	NA	Total
Alabama	Male	0	0	0	0	20	1	0	21
	Female	2	0	6	0	79	3	0	90
	Subtotal	*2*	*0*	*6*	*0*	*99*	*4*	*0*	*111*
Albany	Male	0	0	0	0	27	0	17	44
	Female	0	2	0	1	97	1	51	152
	Subtotal	*0*	*2*	*0*	*1*	*124*	*1*	*68*	*196*
Alberta	Male	—	—	—	—	—	1	17	18
	Female	—	—	—	—	—	4	66	70
	Subtotal	*—*	*—*	*—*	*—*	*—*	*5*	*83*	*88*
Arizona	Male	0	0	0	0	29	5	0	34
	Female	0	3	1	2	91	3	1	101
	Subtotal	*0*	*3*	*1*	*2*	*120*	*8*	*1*	*135*
British Columbia	Male	—	—	—	—	—	2	20	22
	Female	—	—	—	—	—	8	71	79
	Subtotal	*—*	*—*	*—*	*—*	*—*	*10*	*91*	*101*
Buffalo	Male	0	0	1	2	42	2	0	47
	Female	2	0	4	2	132	5	0	145
	Subtotal	*2*	*0*	*5*	*4*	*174*	*7*	*0*	*192*

AI   American Indian or Alaskan Native
AP   Asian or Pacific Islander
B   Black, not of Hispanic origin
H   Hispanic
W   White, not of Hispanic origin
I   International student
NA   No ethnic information available

(Continued)

Table 5-3. Ethnic Distribution of Students in MLS Programs *(Continued)*

School	Gender	AI	AP	B	H	W	I	NA	Total
Calif. Los Angeles	Male	0	1	1	1	27	0	0	30
	Female	0	9	7	4	63	4	0	87
	Subtotal	*0*	*10*	*8*	*5*	*90*	*4*	*0*	*117*
Catholic	Male	0	3	7	2	66	3	0	81
	Female	2	5	35	2	212	11	0	267
	Subtotal	*2*	*8*	*42*	*4*	*278*	*14*	*0*	*348*
Clarion	Male	1	0	0	0	9	5	0	15
	Female	1	1	0	1	63	4	0	70
	Subtotal	*2*	*1*	*0*	*1*	*72*	*9*	*0*	*85*
Clark Atlanta	Male	0	0	14	0	10	5	0	29
	Female	0	0	39	2	18	2	0	61
	Subtotal	*0*	*0*	*53*	*2*	*28*	*7*	*0*	*90*
Dalhousie	Male	0	0	0	0	15	0	0	15
	Female	0	0	1	0	52	3	0	56
	Subtotal	*0*	*0*	*1*	*0*	*67*	*3*	*0*	*71*
Drexel	Male	0	0	0	0	38	1	10	49
	Female	0	5	6	1	146	3	18	179
	Subtotal	*0*	*5*	*6*	*1*	*184*	*4*	*28*	*228*

School	Gender	AI	AP	B	H	W	I	NA	Total
Emporia	Male	1	0	0	1	57	3	0	62
	Female	0	4	4	2	299	9	0	318
	Subtotal	*1*	*4*	*4*	*3*	*356*	*12*	*0*	*380*
Florida State	Male	1	0	1	1	42	2	0	47
	Female	0	3	7	3	171	6	0	190
	Subtotal	*1*	*3*	*8*	*4*	*213*	*8*	*0*	*237*
Hawaii	Male	0	11	0	0	15	2	0	28
	Female	0	48	0	1	25	2	0	76
	Subtotal	*0*	*59*	*0*	*1*	*40*	*4*	*0*	*104*
Illinois	Male	0	2	4	3	58	7	0	74
	Female	0	9	7	2	138	7	0	163
	Subtotal	*0*	*11*	*11*	*5*	*196*	*14*	*0*	*237*
Indiana	Male	0	0	0	1	88	4	3	96
	Female	1	7	6	2	253	14	8	291
	Subtotal	*1*	*7*	*6*	*3*	*341*	*18*	*11*	*387*
Iowa	Male	0	0	1	0	19	0	0	20
	Female	0	1	0	1	67	3	0	72
	Subtotal	*0*	*1*	*1*	*1*	*86*	*3*	*0*	*92*

AI   American Indian or Alaskan Native
AP   Asian or Pacific Islander
B   Black, not of Hispanic origin
H   Hispanic
W   White, not of Hispanic origin
I   International student
NA   No ethnic information available

(Continued)

Table 5-3. Ethnic Distribution of Students in MLS Programs *(Continued)*

School	Gender	AI	AP	B	H	W	I	NA	Total
Kent State	Male	1	1	2	0	87	1	0	92
	Female	0	5	9	2	384	4	0	404
	Subtotal	*1*	*6*	*11*	*2*	*471*	*5*	*0*	*496*
Kentucky	Male	0	1	0	0	51	1	0	53
	Female	0	1	4	1	142	0	1	149
	Subtotal	*0*	*2*	*4*	*1*	*193*	*1*	*1*	*202*
Long Island	Male	0	1	3	0	54	0	0	58
	Female	0	7	9	5	286	1	0	308
	Subtotal	*0*	*8*	*12*	*5*	*340*	*1*	*0*	*366*
Louisiana State	Male	0	0	1	0	21	2	0	24
	Female	0	3	11	3	69	18	1	105
	Subtotal	*0*	*3*	*12*	*3*	*90*	*20*	*1*	*129*
Maryland	Male	0	2	4	0	61	1	0	68
	Female	1	4	9	1	171	1	0	187
	Subtotal	*1*	*6*	*13*	*1*	*232*	*2*	*0*	*255*
McGill	Male	—	—	—	—	—	5	35	40
	Female	—	—	—	—	—	10	81	91
	Subtotal	*—*	*—*	*—*	*—*	*—*	*15*	*116*	*131*

School	Gender	AI	AP	B	H	W	I	NA	Total
Michigan	Male	1	1	1	0	53	0	7	63
	Female	0	14	5	4	129	0	13	165
	Subtotal	*1*	*15*	*6*	*4*	*182*	*0*	*20*	*228*
Missouri	Male	1	1	0	0	34	0	0	36
	Female	0	0	4	0	75	1	0	80
	Subtotal	*1*	*1*	*4*	*0*	*109*	*1*	*0*	*116*
Montréal	Male	0	0	0	0	38	3	0	41
	Female	0	0	0	0	93	4	0	97
	Subtotal	*0*	*0*	*0*	*0*	*131*	*7*	*0*	*138*
NC Central	Male	1	0	3	0	26	8	0	38
	Female	1	3	28	1	95	6	0	134
	Subtotal	*2*	*3*	*31*	*1*	*121*	*14*	*0*	*172*
NC Chapel Hill	Male	1	1	0	1	22	2	0	27
	Female	1	1	4	2	105	1	0	114
	Subtotal	*2*	*2*	*4*	*3*	*127*	*3*	*0*	*141*
NC Greensboro	Male	1	0	1	0	38	0	0	40
	Female	0	3	9	0	162	2	0	176
	Subtotal	*1*	*3*	*10*	*0*	*200*	*2*	*0*	*216*

AI American Indian or Alaskan Native
AP Asian or Pacific Islander
B   Black, not of Hispanic origin
H   Hispanic
W   White, not of Hispanic origin
I   International student
NA No ethnic information available

(Continued)

Table 5-3. Ethnic Distribution of Students in MLS Programs *(Continued)*

School	Gender	AI	AP	B	H	W	I	NA	Total
North Texas	Male	0	3	2	3	48	2	0	58
	Female	0	6	14	6	169	6	7	208
	Subtotal	*0*	*9*	*16*	*9*	*217*	*8*	*7*	*266*
Oklahoma	Male	1	0	0	0	19	1	0	21
	Female	9	0	3	0	100	2	0	114
	Subtotal	*10*	*0*	*3*	*0*	*119*	*3*	*0*	*135*
Pittsburgh	Male	0	0	0	0	36	3	0	39
	Female	0	0	8	0	125	8	0	141
	Subtotal	*0*	*0*	*8*	*0*	*161*	*11*	*0*	*180*
Pratt	Male	0	1	10	6	60	1	0	78
	Female	0	13	28	10	141	5	0	197
	Subtotal	*0*	*14*	*38*	*16*	*201*	*6*	*0*	*275*
Puerto Rico	Male	0	0	0	38	0	1	0	39
	Female	0	0	0	87	0	1	0	88
	Subtotal	*0*	*0*	*0*	*125*	*0*	*2*	*0*	*127*
Queens	Male	0	5	8	5	79	4	0	101
	Female	0	23	21	12	203	6	0	265
	Subtotal	*0*	*28*	*29*	*17*	*282*	*10*	*0*	*366*

School	Gender	AI	AP	B	H	W	I	NA	Total
Rhode Island	Male	0	0	0	0	34	0	0	34
	Female	0	1	0	0	137	1	0	139
	Subtotal	*0*	*1*	*0*	*0*	*171*	*1*	*0*	*173*
Rosary (now Dominican)	Male	0	1	1	2	61	4	5	74
	Female	0	6	7	5	305	9	5	337
	Subtotal	*0*	*7*	*8*	*7*	*366*	*13*	*10*	*411*
Rutgers	Male	1	2	1	1	54	2	2	63
	Female	0	11	9	5	224	5	5	259
	Subtotal	*1*	*13*	*10*	*6*	*278*	*7*	*7*	*322*
St. John's	Male	0	1	5	0	17	2	0	25
	Female	0	5	11	6	52	2	0	76
	Subtotal	*0*	*6*	*16*	*6*	*69*	*4*	*0*	*101*
San Jose	Male	14	14	3	7	69	1	51	159
	Female	53	30	15	16	233	2	130	479
	Subtotal	*67*	*44*	*18*	*23*	*302*	*3*	*181*	*638*
Simmons	Male	0	0	0	0	73	1	0	74
	Female	0	6	5	2	350	9	0	372
	Subtotal	*0*	*6*	*5*	*2*	*423*	*10*	*0*	*446*

AI   American Indian or Alaskan Native
AP   Asian or Pacific Islander
B   Black, not of Hispanic origin
H   Hispanic
W   White, not of Hispanic origin
I   International student
NA   No ethnic information available

(Continued)

Table 5-3. Ethnic Distribution of Students in MLS Programs *(Continued)*

School	Gender	AI	AP	B	H	W	I	NA	Total
South Carolina	Male	2	0	3	2	62	4	0	73
	Female	1	6	21	0	334	7	2	371
	Subtotal	*3*	*6*	*24*	*2*	*396*	*11*	*2*	*444*
South Florida	Male	0	0	4	6	41	0	0	51
	Female	0	4	8	10	175	3	0	200
	Subtotal	*0*	*4*	*12*	*16*	*216*	*3*	*0*	*251*
Southern Connecticut	Male	0	0	0	0	28	0	3	31
	Female	0	2	1	1	124	0	11	139
	Subtotal	*0*	*2*	*1*	*1*	*152*	*0*	*14*	*170*
Southern Mississippi	Male	0	0	0	0	11	2	0	13
	Female	0	2	6	0	58	3	0	69
	Subtotal	*0*	*2*	*6*	*0*	*69*	*5*	*0*	*82*
Syracuse	Male	0	0	1	0	32	1	0	34
	Female	0	1	0	0	113	14	0	128
	Subtotal	*0*	*1*	*1*	*0*	*145*	*15*	*0*	*162*
Tennessee	Male	0	0	0	0	46	3	0	49
	Female	0	1	2	0	153	8	0	164
	Subtotal	*0*	*1*	*2*	*0*	*199*	*11*	*0*	*213*

School	Gender	AI	AP	B	H	W	I	NA	Total
Texas	Male	1	0	3	10	86	4	0	104
	Female	1	3	3	28	250	7	0	292
	Subtotal	*2*	*3*	*6*	*38*	*336*	*11*	*0*	*396*
Texas Woman's	Male	0	1	0	1	15	0	0	17
	Female	1	5	12	2	203	2	0	225
	Subtotal	*1*	*6*	*12*	*3*	*218*	*2*	*0*	*242*
Toronto	Male	—	—	—	—	—	6	55	61
	Female	—	—	—	—	—	16	170	186
	Subtotal	*—*	*—*	*—*	*—*	*—*	*22*	*225*	*247*
Washington	Male	0	5	2	2	31	3	0	43
	Female	3	5	5	0	131	0	0	144
	Subtotal	*3*	*10*	*7*	*2*	*162*	*3*	*0*	*187*
Wayne State	Male	1	0	4	0	90	0	3	98
	Female	2	9	25	4	275	0	1	316
	Subtotal	*3*	*9*	*29*	*4*	*365*	*0*	*4*	*414*
Western Ontario	Male	—	—	—	—	—	0	55	55
	Female	—	—	—	—	—	0	141	141
	Subtotal	*—*	*—*	*—*	*—*	*—*	*0*	*196*	*196*

AI American Indian or Alaskan Native
AP Asian or Pacific Islander
B Black, not of Hispanic origin
H Hispanic
W White, not of Hispanic origin
I International student
NA No ethnic information available

(Continued)

Table 5-3. Ethnic Distribution of Students in MLS Programs *(Continued)*

School	Gender	AI	AP	B	H	W	I	NA	Total
Wisc. Madison	Male	0	0	0	0	42	1	0	43
	Female	0	2	2	1	119	4	0	128
	Subtotal	*0*	*2*	*2*	*1*	*161*	*5*	*0*	*171*
Wisc. Milwaukee	Male	0	0	0	1	40	3	7	51
	Female	2	2	7	0	176	7	0	194
	Subtotal	*2*	*2*	*7*	*1*	*216*	*10*	*7*	*245*
Total (56 schools)	Male	29	58	91	96	2,121	115	290	2,800
	Female	83	281	428	240	7,767	267	783	9,849
	Total	*112*	*339*	*519*	*336*	*9,888*	*382*	*1,073*	*12,649*
Mean (n = 51)	Male	0.57	1.14	1.78	1.88	41.59	2.05		50.00
	Female	1.63	5.51	8.39	4.71	152.29	4.77		175.88
	Total	*2.20*	*6.65*	*10.17*	*6.59*	*193.88*	*6.82* (n = 56)		*225.88* (n = 56)

AI   American Indian or Alaskan Native
AP   Asian or Pacific Islander
B   Black, not of Hispanic origin
H   Hispanic
W   White, not of Hispanic origin
I   International student
NA   No ethnic information available

Table 5-4. Ethnic Background of Library Faculty

Rank	American Indian	Asian or Pacific Islander	Black	Hispanic	White	Total
Deans and Directors	0	1	3	2	42	48
Professors	0	5	6	4	119	134
Associate Professors	2	7	7	2	154	172
Assistant Professors	1	16	16	4	110	147
Instructors	0	0	0	0	16	16
Lecturers	0	0	2	0	14	16
Total	3	29	34	12	455	533
Percent of Total	0.5	5.4	6.4	2.2	85.4	

NOTES

1. Prudence W. Dalrymple, "The State of the Schools," *American Libraries* 28 (Jan. 1997): 31.
2. Nathan Glazer, "In Defense of Preference," *New Republic* 218 (April 6, 1998): 18.
3. Dinesh D'Souza, "Sins of Admissions," *New Republic* 204 (Feb. 18, 1991): 30.
4. Glazer, "In Defense of Preference," p. 18.
5. "Statistical Report," *Library and Information Science Education*, ed. Evelyn H. Daniel and Jerry D. Saye (Arlington, Va.: Association for Library and Information Science Education, 1997), 69–71.
6. Ibid., 25.

Bibliography

Articles

Alire, Camila A. "Ethnic Populations: A Model for Statewide Service." *American Libraries* 28 (Nov. 1997): 38.

———. "Mentoring on My Mind: It Takes a Family to Graduate a Minority Library Professional." *American Libraries* 28 (Nov. 1997): 41–43.

———. "Walking the Walk: The Colorado Perspective." ALA Chapter Relations Committee, Colorado Council on Library Development, Committee on Library Services to Ethnic Populations, 1996.

Bahls, Jane Easter. "Culture Shock." *Entrepreneur* 22 (Feb. 1994): 66.

Barnes, Julian E. "Battle Widens over College Affirmative Action." *U.S. News & World Report* 123 (Dec. 22, 1997): 7–8.

Bell, Chip R. "A New Key to Employee Loyalty: Portable Wisdom (Mentors in a Corporate Environment)." *Management Review* 85 (Dec. 1996): 20.

Bergheim, Kim. "Reaching Out to Minorities." *Outlook* 58 (winter 1991): 24.

Bunzel, John H. "Race and College Admissions." *Public Interest* (winter 1996): 49.

Burgess, David R. "Barriers to Graduate School for Minority-Group Students." *Chronicle of Higher Education* 44 (Oct. 10, 1997): B7.

Case, Tony. "Remember Newsroom Diversity?" *Editor & Publisher* 130 (Feb. 22, 1997): 15.

Cohen, Adam. "The Next Great Battle over Affirmative Action." *Time* 150 (Nov. 10, 1997): 52.

Cohen, Carl. "Race, Lies, and Hopwood." *Commentary* 101 (June 1996): 39.

Cronin, Blaise, Michael Stiffler, and Dorothy Day. "The Emergent Market for Information Professionals: Educational Opportunities and Implications." *Library Trends* 24 (fall 1993): 257.

Crowley, Aileen. "High-School Heroes." *PC Week* 15 (April 13, 1998): 69.

Dalrymple, Prudence. "The State of the Schools." *American Libraries* 28 (Jan. 1997): 31.

"Diversity, Perceptions of Equity, and Communicative Openness in the Workplace." *Journal of Business Communication* 33 (special issue: "Diversity in the Workplace") (Oct. 1996): 443.

Dryfus, Joel. "Get Ready for the New Work Force." *Fortune* 121 (April 23, 1990): 165.

D'Souza, Dinesh. "Sins of Admission." *New Republic* 204 (Feb. 18, 1991): 30.

Dyer, Esther, and Concha Robertson-Kozan. "Hispanics in the U.S." *School Library Journal* 29 (April 1983): 27.

Fickenscher, Lisa. "Are You Marketing to Groups?" *American Banker* 158 (Nov. 10, 1993): 20.

Gaillard, Mazi. "Is the Pot Melting?" *Footwear News* 52 (Aug. 12, 1996): 40.

Glazer, Nathan. "In Defense of Preference." *New Republic* 218 (April 6, 1998): 18.

Hanamura, Steve. "Working with People Who Are Different." *Training & Development Journal* 43 (June 1989): 110.

Haukoos, Gerry D., and Archie B. Beauvais. "Creating Positive Cultural Images: Thoughts for Teaching about American Indians." *Childhood Education* 73 (winter 1996): 77.

Herren, Laura M. "The New Game of HR: Playing to Win." *Personnel* 66 (June 1989): 18.

Hoffman, Nancy. "Shifting Gears: How to Get Results with Affirmative Action." *Change* 25 (March-April 1993): 30.

Hopkins, Willie E., and Shirley A. Hopkins. "Getting the Jump on Work Force 2000: Some Helpful Hints for Managers." *Management Quarterly* 32 (fall 1991): 33.

Jordan, Kenneth A., Mitchell F. Rice, and Audrey Mathews. "Educating Minorities for Public Service in the Year 2000." *Public Manager: The New Bureaucrat* 23 (summer 1994): 51.

Josey, E. J. "Minority Representation in Library and Information Science Programs." *Bookmark* 48 (fall 1989): 1.

Kaplowitz, Joan et al. "Mentoring Library School Students—A Survey." *Special Libraries* 83 (fall 1992): 219.

Kent, Susan Goldberg. "American Public Libraries." *Daedalus* 125 (fall 1996): 207.

Knowles, Em Claire, and Linda Jolivet. "Recruiting the Underrepresented: Collaborative Efforts between Library Educators and Library Practitioners." *Library Administration & Management* 5 (fall 1991): 189.

Leo, John. "The Luring of Black Students." *U.S. News & World Report* 114 (March 15, 1993): 20.

Lewis, Anne C. "Minority Teachers." *Education Digest* 59 (Jan. 1994): 60.

Light, Paul. "Not like Us." *Journal of Policy Analysis & Management* 13 (winter 1994): 164.

McCook, Kathleen de la Peña, Kate Lippincott, and Bob Woodard. "Planning for a Diverse Workforce in Library and Information Science Professions." Research study conducted at the University of South Florida, 1997.

Martinez, Elizabeth. "Diversity: The Twenty-First-Century Spectrum." *American Libraries* 28 (March 1997): 32.

"Me! A Librarian!" Ohio State Library and Library Council of Ohio, 1998. Recruitment brochure.

Miles, Laureen. "The Right Thing." *Mediaweek* 2 (Oct. 19, 1992): 16.

Morton, Linda P. "Targeting Minority Publics." *Public Relations Quarterly* 42 (summer 1997): 23.

O'Connor, Brian Wright. "Are Advertising Agencies Serious about Hiring African Americans?" *Black Enterprise* 23 (March 1993): 88.

Piercynski, Mary, Myrna Matranga, and Gary Peltier. "Legislative Appropriation for Minority Teacher Recruitment: Did It Really Matter?" *The Clearing House* 70 (March-April 1997): 205.

Quezada, Shelly. "Mainstreaming Library Services to Multicultural Populations." *Wilson Library Bulletin* 66 (Feb. 1992): 28.

Reid, Calvin, and Tanya Padgett. "Houses with No Doors." *Publishers Weekly* 241 (May 23, 1994): 62.

Sanoff, Alvin P. "Did They Admit Me?" *U.S. News & World Report* 122 (April 14, 1997): 48.

Schwartz, Joe, and Thomas Exter. "All Our Children." *American Demographics* 11 (May 1989): 34.

Smith, Bob. "Executive Development Begins in High School." *HR Focus* 71 (April 1994): 7.

——— "Recruitment Insights for Strategic Workforce Diversity." *HR Focus* 71 (Jan. 1994): 7.

Sowell, Thomas. "Damaging Admissions." *Forbes* 156 (Oct. 23, 1995): 121.

Speer, Tibbett L. "Libraries from A to Z." *American Demographics* 17 (Sept. 1995): 48.

"Supreme Court Refuses to Rule on Race-Based College Admissions." *Jet* 90 (July 22, 1996): 14.

Tifft, Susan. "The Search for Minorities: Despite Increased Wooing, Few Go On to College." *Time* 134 (Aug. 21, 1989): 64.

Van Collie, Shimon-Craig. "Moving Up through Mentoring." *Workforce* 77 (March 1998): 36.

Wheeler, Maurice B., and Jaqueline Hanson. "Improving Diversity: Recruiting Students to the Library Profession." *Journal of Library Administration* 21 (July-Aug. 1995): 137.

Whitwell, Stuart C. A. "Intimate World, Intimate Workplace: How the Association of Research Libraries and ALA Are Strengthening Their Commitment to Diversity." *American Libraries* 27 (Feb. 1996): 56.

Williams, Wilda W. "You Can Take Your MLS out of the Library." *Library Journal* 119 (Nov. 12, 1994): 43.

Woodsworth, Anne. "Librarianship: The Hot Profession." *Library Journal* 122 (Oct. 15, 1997): 42.

Books

Landen, Hal. *Marketing with Video.* New York: Oak Tree Press, 1996.

Levinson, Jay, and Seth Godin. *The Guerrilla Marketing Handbook.* Boston: Houghton, 1994.

Moen, William E., and Kathleen Heim, eds. *Librarians for the New Millennium.* Chicago and London: American Library Association, 1988.

Schaaf, Dick. *Keeping the Edge.* New York: Dutton, 1995.

Treacy, Michael, and Fred Wiersema. *The Discipline of Market Leaders.* Reading, Mass: Addison-Wesley, 1995.

Weingand, Darlene E. *Customer Service Excellence.* Chicago and London: American Library Association, 1997.

Index

Page references in italics refer to figures and tables

Gregory L. Reese, a native of Cleveland, Ohio, received his undergraduate degree in history from Morehouse College, Atlanta, Georgia, and his Master of Library Science degree from Case Western Reserve University, Cleveland, Ohio. During the past 23 years, Reese has served in several capacities of public librarianship and is presently director of the East Cleveland Public Library, East Cleveland, Ohio. Very active on both the local and national levels of the profession, Reese has served on numerous committees of the Public Library Association and the American Library Association. He is currently President of the Black Caucus of the American Library Association. Reese is a founding member of the Cleveland Area African American Library Association (CAALA) and was selected Ohio's Librarian of the Year in 1991.

Ernestine L. Hawkins received her undergraduate degree from Miami University, Oxford, Ohio, and her Master of Library Science degree from Case Western Reserve University, Cleveland, Ohio. She has been a librarian and administrator for over twenty years. She is currently the deputy director of the East Cleveland Public Library. Hawkins has served on or chaired committees of both the American Library Association and the Public Library Association. She was one of the founding members, and the first elected president, of the Cleveland Area African American Library Association (CAALA) and was recently elected to the Executive Board of the Black Caucus of the American Library Association.